Revitalizing Arts Education Through Community-Wide Coordination

Susan J. Bodilly
Catherine H. Augustine
with Laura Zakaras

Commissioned by

The Wallace Foundation

Supporting ideas.
Sharing solutions.
Expanding opportunities.

 RESEARCH IN THE ARTS

The research in this report was produced within RAND Education, a unit of the RAND Corporation. The research was commissioned by The Wallace Foundation.

Library of Congress Cataloging-in-Publication Data

Bodilly, Susan J.
    Revitalizing arts education through community-wide coordination /
Susan J. Bodilly, Catherine H. Augustine, with Laura Zakaras.
        p. cm.
    Includes bibliographical references.
    ISBN 978-0-8330-4306-1 (pbk. : alk. paper)
    1. Art—Study and teaching—United States. 2. Community and school—United
States. I. Augustine, Catherine H., 1968– II. Zakaras, Laura. III. Title.

N350.B634 2009
700.71'073—dc22

                                                                    2008006853

The RAND Corporation is a nonprofit research organization providing objective analysis and effective solutions that address the challenges facing the public and private sectors around the world. RAND's publications do not necessarily reflect the opinions of its research clients and sponsors.

RAND® is a registered trademark.

Cover design by Eileen Delson La Russo

Published 2008 by the RAND Corporation
1776 Main Street, P.O. Box 2138, Santa Monica, CA 90407-2138
1200 South Hayes Street, Arlington, VA 22202-5050
4570 Fifth Avenue, Suite 600, Pittsburgh, PA 15213
RAND URL: http://www.rand.org/
To order RAND documents or to obtain additional information, contact
Distribution Services: Telephone: (310) 451-7002;
Fax: (310) 451-6915; Email: order@rand.org

Preface

For more than 30 years, arts education has struggled to maintain space and time in publicly funded education in the United States for children in kindergarten through grade 12. In the nation's urban centers, reductions in state and local budgets in the 1970s and 1980s led to diminished arts programming in favor of maintaining other subjects. More recently, government-legislated accountability based on mathematics and reading test scores has shifted attention to these subjects, to the detriment of other elements of the curriculum.

Despite these trends, some urban communities have not given up the struggle to preserve arts education, and have sought to improve children's access to quality arts learning experiences through collaboration and coordination among the different providers and influencers of arts education. This report examines efforts by six communities to improve arts education provision in their regions through collaborative means. Concrete examples are given to answer why and how these efforts have unfolded and to document the associated challenges.

The audience for this report consists of persons interested in improving arts education in urban U.S. centers. As such, it includes leaders in public school districts, mayoral offices, foundations, community-based providers of arts learning activities, out-of-school-time providers of such activities, and cultural centers; it also includes teachers and artists. Federal and state arts and education policymakers may also find the report of interest.

This study was conducted by RAND Education, a unit of the RAND Corporation. The work was commissioned by The Wallace Foundation, which seeks to support and share effective ideas and practices that expand learning and enrichment opportunities for all people. The foundation's three current objectives are to strengthen education leadership to improve student achievement, to improve after-school learning opportunities, and to build appreciation and demand for the arts.

The Wallace Foundation has funded a separate study to examine reputedly high-quality arts education programs to understand what "quality arts learning" means to those who provide the programs and how they achieve and sustain it. That study is being undertaken by Harvard's Project Zero under the leadership of Steven Seidel.

Other RAND Books on the Arts

Cultivating Demand for the Arts: Arts Learning, Arts Engagement, and State Arts Policy (2008)
Laura Zakaras, Julia F. Lowell

Arts and Culture in the Metropolis: Strategies for Sustainability (2007)
Kevin F. McCarthy, Elizabeth Heneghan Ondaatje,
Jennifer L. Novak

The Arts and State Governments: At Arm's Length or Arm in Arm? (2006)
Julia F. Lowell, Elizabeth Heneghan Ondaatje

A Portrait of the Visual Arts: Meeting the Challenges of a New Era (2005)
Kevin F. McCarthy, Elizabeth Heneghan Ondaatje,
Arthur Brooks, Andras Szanto

Gifts of the Muse: Reframing the Debate About the Benefits of the Arts (2004)
Kevin F. McCarthy, Elizabeth Heneghan Ondaatje,
Laura Zakaras, Arthur Brooks

Arts Education Partnerships: Lessons Learned from One School District's Experience (2004)
Melissa K. Rowe, Laura Werber Castaneda,
Tessa Kaganoff, Abby Robyn

State Arts Agencies, 1965–2003: Whose Interests to Serve? (2004)
Julia Lowell

From Celluloid to Cyberspace: The Media Arts and the Changing Arts World (2002)
Kevin F. McCarthy, Elizabeth H. Ondaatje

The Performing Arts in a New Era (2001)
Kevin F. McCarthy, Arthur Brooks,
Julia Lowell, Laura Zakaras

A New Framework for Building Participation in the Arts (2001)
Kevin F. McCarthy, Kimberly Jinnett

Contents

Figures and Tables

Figures

Tables

Summary

Arts education has been a low priority in the nation's public schools for more than 30 years. Reports from the late 1970s and 1980s reveal that students received little arts instruction at any grade level, and that what they did receive was typically casual and spotty. Severe fiscal crises in America's urban centers in those years exacerbated the situation as schools responded by cutting teaching positions, particularly those considered to be outside core subject areas. More recently, the arts have had difficulty keeping even a tenuous foothold in many urban schools because of general education reforms, such as the No Child Left Behind Act, that hold schools accountable for standardized test scores in mathematics and reading. In addition, site-based management, designed to boost academic achievement by giving principals ultimate authority over school curriculum, has in some cases created a formidable obstacle to increasing access to arts education in urban school districts.

In some urban centers, a countermovement to this dwindling presence of arts education in the schools has developed in the form of initiatives aimed at coordinating schools, cultural institutions, community-based organizations, foundations, and/or government agencies to promote access to arts learning for children in and outside of school. Our study examined this phenomenon in six metropolitan areas across the nation. The evidence we gathered about these communities' coordinated arts learning efforts shows some signs of progress but is also cautionary. In light of the historical factors that have impeded access to arts learning in the past, it is apparent that the efforts we investigated are, generally speaking, fragile. To succeed in the long run, such efforts must have committed and sustained leadership, sufficient resources, and a policy context that allows them to survive.

Purpose and Approach

The purpose of our research, which was sponsored by The Wallace Foundation, was to analyze how local arts education initiatives across multiple organizations were started, how they evolved, what kinds of organizations became involved, what conditions fostered or impeded coordination among those organizations, and what strategies were developed to improve both access to and quality of arts education in the communities. In other words, our purpose was not to evaluate the success of these initiatives, but to descriptively and comparatively analyze their formation and evolution. We also analyzed historical trends in arts education over the past few decades to understand the conditions motivating these initiatives.

Our approach involved several steps. First, we reviewed the relevant literature and conducted extended interviews with nationally recognized experts on arts education to improve our understanding of the prevailing issues in the field and to gather recommendations on which sites were the most promising for study. This process helped us select six sites that reportedly were actively engaged in developing complex local arts education networks: Alameda County (which includes the cities of Oakland and Berkeley) in Northern California, Boston, Chicago, Dallas, Los Angeles County, and New York City.

At the same time, we identified major attributes of effective systems by drawing from the literature in various fields: systems development, coordinated delivery systems in the social services, and partnerships in delivering arts education. This step helped us build our interview protocols and analyze our findings.

Finally, we performed a comparative case-study analysis based on site visits, a document review, and interviews with about 120 participants across the six sites.

Motivation for Change

Because of the pervasive neglect of arts education in the kindergarten through grade 12 (K–12) public school system, most children are given only a smattering of arts instruction, and some are given none at all. Access to arts education, which is rarely documented, appears to be highly uneven. Surveys conducted in the sites we studied revealed striking inequities: While some schools had an established record of exceptional courses in the arts, other schools had few offerings or none.

Over the years, the difficulty of garnering policy support and resources for arts education in the schools brought outside providers of arts learning opportunities into the picture. Cultural organizations began offering more arts education programs to children, and, more recently, two other types of providers have proliferated: out-of-school-time (OST) organizations (such as city departments of parks and recreation and YMCAs) and community-based organizations (such as Young Audiences, the nationwide nonprofit founded to connect professional artists with students and teachers in schools). Beyond these organizations are a host of others, which we call *influencers*, that have taken steps to promote more arts learning: private foundations and business leaders, state and local arts agencies and city cultural affairs offices, and higher education institutions that prepare classroom teachers and arts specialists and offer professional development in arts education. This proliferation of players has created a highly complex arts education ecology.

It is against this background that some communities have committed to building a coordinated network of providers and influencers to revive arts learning. The leaders of these coordinated efforts believe that by combining forces to accomplish a shared goal, they will not only gain greater leverage against the prevailing trends in arts education, but will also be more-effective advocates for the arts and command more resources for providing more and better arts education to children.

Patterns

Four patterns can be used to describe how community leaders in our six case-study sites approached the issue of arts education, located arts education within the community, coordinated and involved other organizations, and progressed toward their goals:

The Alameda County and Los Angeles County sites focused on expanding school-based arts education. In both cases, county offices (through the Alliance for Arts Learning Leadership in Alameda County and Arts for All in Los Angeles County) played the lead in network building. Stakeholder participation was highly diverse, and numerous school districts joined with cultural institutions and community-based organizations, as well as with influencers in government, higher education, philanthropy, and business, in well-established efforts.

The Boston site focused on increasing the access of at-risk youth to OST programs, a few of which were arts based. Coordination, which was just emerging at the time of our study, was among the mayor's office, local foundations, business leaders, and a public-private partnership called Boston After School and Beyond.

The Chicago and New York City sites focused on changing policy at the district level to facilitate sequential arts education in the schools during the school day. Coordination was primarily led by the citywide school district office and did not heavily involve the many other possible participants in the city as equal partners in expanding access to arts education. Multi-organization coordination outside of routine contractual relationships was thus nascent in these two sites.

The Dallas site focused on improving access to both in-school and OST arts learning programs. Coordination developed through the initiative of a community-based organization, Young Audiences of North Texas. In 1997, ArtsPartners, an outgrowth of Young Audiences, was created as a public-private partnership to provide integrated arts learning to all elementary students in the Dallas Independent School District with funding from the city, district, and private donors. In 2004, this organization was reorganized, expanded, and renamed Big Thought. Focusing at the elementary level, it successfully expanded access across all schools and begam offering programs to families in several neighborhoods throughout the city.

Common Strategies

We found that despite the differences in their coordination efforts, the six sites used many of the same strategies to improve access to arts education:

- *Conducting audits of arts education.* Five sites had conducted surveys to benchmark the state of arts education in the schools. In all cases, the surveys illustrated profound inequities that helped galvanize support for the initiatives.
- *Setting a goal of access for all.* Five sites had set this goal. Some, however (for example, Dallas), had chosen to support access for all but to initially focus on elementary school children. Their argument was that as these children moved up through the system, they and their families would become the best advocates for arts education improvements in the higher grades. The Boston site focused on out-of-school-provision for at-risk children.
- *Strategic planning.* Five of the sites were in the midst of strategic planning efforts, often funded by foundations.
- *Constructing a case.* Three sites had spent considerable time developing arguments about the benefits of arts education in order to attract organizations into their collaborative and reach out to the public. One had hired a professional case-making firm for this purpose.
- *Attracting and leveraging resources.* Five sites had developed innovative approaches to funding that included leveraging and pooling funds. For example, in Dallas, Big Thought successfully leveraged funding from local and national sources. In Chicago, 17 local foundations and individuals joined together to fund half the salary for three years of a new position for a fine arts advocate for the school district. And in Los Angeles, Arts for All created a pooled fund. Each year, ten to 15 organizations contributed to the pool, and contributors sat on a board that met quarterly to determine how to spend the money. The sixth site, New York City, took a more traditional route to funding by relying on government money. When a policy shift toward site-based management later caused categorical arts funding to go away, their coordination efforts were inhibited.
- *Hiring an arts education coordinator highly placed within the school district administration.* All six sites had or were urging placement of an arts education coordinator in the school systems' central offices to advocate for the arts and secure a place for them in the district's core curriculum. Moreover, rather than hiring a teacher to perform as the coordinator part time (a more traditional approach), each site either already had or was advocating for hiring a senior, full-time person for the arts leadership role within the district.
- *Building individual and organizational capacity.* A key strategy of all six sites was to build the capacity of arts teachers, regular classroom teachers, and teaching artists

to deliver high-quality arts learning, and to develop principals and other administrators capable of planning and supporting such learning in their organizations.

- *Advocating.* Because of the extensive forces aligned against them, all six sites had been or were advocating for arts education on multiple fronts: with superintendents, principals, teachers, and OST coordinators on one hand; with parents and local and state policymakers on the other. Some sites also had been or were working closely with formal advocacy organizations that track local school-district elections and/or urge increased state funding for arts education.

All six sites focused more on expanding access to arts learning than on improving the quality of arts learning activities. However, all of them took a number of steps to improve quality—for example,

- requiring that curriculum be aligned with state arts standards
- developing curriculum frameworks and arts assessment tools
- qualifying programs offered by providers outside the schools
- putting in place peer modeling, review, and ranking.

Factors That Foster and Impede Coordination

In addition to common strategies, we identified specific factors that foster coordination and that impede it. In the early stages of the coordination effort, the fostering factors are convening key stakeholders to build support, overcoming ideological differences, identifying local leadership talent, and laying the groundwork for subsequent coordination. Initial seed funding for collaboration is another factor considered important for getting community-wide efforts off the ground. Once the effort is further along, the important fostering factors are acquiring sustained funding, convening and joint planning, and engaging in a process of evaluation, feedback, and improvement to ensure advancement toward goals. But perhaps the most important factor in building and maintaining the effort is effective leadership—that is, leaders that are capable, inclusive in style, and stable over time.

The finding that effective leadership is so crucial is not at all surprising: The obstacles to achieving the set goals and the difficulties of coordinating many partners are enormous. The sites found to have made the most progress were those whose leaders were capable (offered legitimate leadership to the effort), inclusive in style (desirous of including diverse organizations), and stable (dedicated to the mission, committed to staying the course). Typical of these leaders was that they did not just welcome diverse stakeholders to the table, they deliberately recruited them.

The factors that impede coordination are largely mirror images of those that foster coordination. They include lack of resources for collaboration, turnover of key leaders, and policies and incentives that prioritize other subjects.

Potential of Coordinated Networks

The struggle to more fully and richly infuse the arts into children's learning experiences involves daunting challenges, such as finding time and space for arts instruction in children's day; securing the support of parents, teachers, principals, funders, policymakers, and others for arts learning; providing professional training in the face of routine turnovers of staff and leaders in public and community-based organizations; dealing with the persistent scarcity of resources; and replacing general policies that continue to marginalize the arts. And despite best efforts, some involved in this struggle have seen progress made over a period of years disappear, wiped out by an abrupt shift in local political leadership or education policy.

Yet even the difficulty of the struggle and the preponderance of setbacks did not keep the coordinated efforts in some of our sites from emerging as a powerful way to change a community's perceptions of the value of arts learning and to strengthen its commitment to extending arts learning to all children. Rather than individually pursuing improved provision of arts learning for children, those who participated in these initiatives worked together as one dedicated crew. Certainly, a policy shift toward better support of arts education would be a welcome aid in the struggle, lessening its difficulty. But until that shift occurs, coordinated efforts across multiple organizations show promise for making a decided impact.

Acknowledgments

Many people helped in conducting this study and producing this report. We would like to thank those at The Wallace Foundation for their substantive and financial support. In particular, Ann Stone and Edward Pauly provided valuable guidance on the intellectual and analytic components of our work. Catherine Fukushima and Dara Rose provided guidance on interviewee selection.

Representatives from each of the six urban communities involved in our case studies were extremely helpful in identifying and enabling access to those persons most knowledgeable about increasing access to arts learning experiences. We would especially like to thank Louise Music, Klare Shaw, Sarah Solotaroff, Frank Quinn, Gigi Antoni, and Sarah Calderon.

We are particularly grateful for the time given to us by our interviewees—both the experts we interviewed when we launched this project and those we interviewed at each of the six sites. Although we are keeping their identities confidential, their insights, opinions, and ideas formed the basis of this document. Steven Seidel of Harvard's Project Zero, Gerri Spilka of OMG, and Richard Deasy of the Arts Education Partnership also provided important insights on our work.

Sharon Koga supported this project through her adept scheduling of interviews across the six sites. Jennifer Novak, Alice Taylor, and Dahlia Lichter devoted much time and effort to interviewing and to taking notes.

The document itself was greatly improved through the efforts of reviewers and editors. In particular, RAND colleague Julia Lowell provided essential insights that led to significant improvements in the document, and Jeri O'Donnell provided essential editing services.

Abbreviations

BASB	Boston After School and Beyond
CAE	Center for Arts Education
CAPE	Chicago Arts Partnerships in Education
DALI	Dallas Arts Learning Initiative
MAP	Model Arts Programming
NAEP	National Assessment of Educational Progress
NCES	National Center for Education Statistics
NCLB	No Child Left Behind Act
NEA	National Endowment for the Arts
OST	out-of-school time

CHAPTER ONE

Introduction

Arts education in the nation's schools is clearly in a state of decline (von Zastrow and Janc, 2004; Rowe et al., 2004; Hamilton et al., 2007; McMurrer, 2007; Woodworth, Gallagher, and Guha, 2007; West, 2007). For many communities, the decline started with significant public budget shortfalls in the 1970s and 1980s that led school districts to drastically cut programs deemed not as central to the academic mission. More recently, the test-based accountability mechanisms of state standards-based reforms and the federal No Child Left Behind Act of 2001 (Public Law 107-110, 2002), commonly known as NCLB, caused schools to focus on the subjects that were to be tested, reading and mathematics, at the expense of other subjects. And many non-tested curriculum areas have been stripped of resources—especially time during the school day—in an effort to meet legislated goals. Attempts to recover from the budget-related declines in arts education are stymied by a prevailing emphasis on other subjects in the schools. Some families have turned to the informal education system for arts education opportunities, but these are often available only to people with the will and resources to access them (Bodilly and Beckett, 2005). Moreover, these outside-the-school arts opportunities must compete with other after-school activities, such as sports and the more generally available forms of entertainment.

A countermovement to this decline of arts education has developed in several locales. On the smallest scale, it may take the form of a partnership between a local performing arts theater and a school to encourage a few performances per year and talks between performers and students. On a larger scale, it may mean developing coordinated initiatives across a community's provider organizations and other stakeholders to bring arts education opportunities to all students. These initiatives can be aimed at delivering arts learning in different ways, such as through sequential courses in school, integration of the arts with other subjects in school, and increased opportunities for participation in outside-the-school programs.

Little has been documented about the practical aspects of creating coordinated initiatives to improve arts education delivery at the local level. Some studies, such as one whose results were published by the Arts Education Partnership and the President's Committee on the Arts and the Humanities (Fiske, 1999), describe arts programs within schools but do not look at more broadly based efforts across whole communities. Others, such as Bodilly et al., 2004, analyze collaborative approaches to education reform but not specifically arts education reform. Still others, such as Rowe et al., 2004, examine the challenges of achieving successful arts education partnerships but do not take a community-wide view.

The rest of this chapter presents information on our study that serves as a foundation for later chapters. We begin by describing the purpose of our study, discussing the methods we used to explore the topic, and providing important background information on both the struggles faced by those attempting to find a place in children's education for arts learning and the debate about how arts education should be provided. We then offer some ideas about what coordinated initiatives might look like and describe this monograph's organization.

Purpose

The Wallace Foundation, a major supporter of efforts to expand participation in the arts, approached RAND about providing a descriptive analysis of community-based collaborative efforts to improve opportunities for high-quality arts learning for children.[1,2] The purpose of the study was to examine the evolution of coordinated approaches to local arts education provision in six sites, focusing on how local assets were deliberately aligned to maximize collective effectiveness and the challenges faced by these efforts. Specifically, we addressed the following questions:

- What does the ecology of local arts education generally look like? How did it evolve?
- Why and how have some sites developed more-coordinated approaches to provision?
- What strategies do these local coordinated groups use to improve access to and quality of arts learning experiences?
- What factors foster and what factors impede these coordinated approaches?

Based on discussions with the foundation, we took the words *to improve opportunities for high-quality arts learning* to mean increase access, ensure more equitable access, improve quality of provision, or improve efficiency of provision. And we assumed that *learning* took place both in school and outside of school. We defined a *community* as

---

[1]   We use *arts education* and *arts learning* interchangeably in this monograph to mean learning related to dance, music, theater, and visual arts. In addition, we assert that arts education and arts learning occur not just in school, but in multiple locations and contexts.

[2]   We use the term *children* in this monograph to mean children who are in kindergarten through grade 12 (K–12).

an entity that was geographically based in a city or county and included schools and districts of education, arts organizations, cultural organizations, parents, community-based organizations, outside-of-school providers, and private funders. *Coordination* was taken to mean deliberate collaboration of these organizations and stakeholders, outside of normal contractual relationships, to provide greater arts education opportunities than would exist without this collaboration. We focused solely on coordination initiatives and thus did not consider individual providers of arts instruction (the many music, vocal, and painting instructors who make a living in the private market) and did not attempt to audit the full range of providers within each community. We also did not assess the value of using coordinated approaches rather than other means to improve arts education.

Methods

This report describes our comparative analysis of six case studies of coordination efforts aimed at improving access to arts learning. Our sources of information were expert interviews, a literature review, and both interviews and document reviews at our chosen sites. We also used the literature to develop a set of attributes of multi-organizational coordination to guide our investigation.

For our initial interviews, we chose 24 nationally known experts on arts education and issues associated with its provision. They included representatives of national arts education associations, state arts agencies, and foundations; and professors, consultants, and providers of arts education experiences. We asked them for materials on the scope of arts education provision and related issues, as well as recommendations of sites attempting to coordinate arts learning provision that might serve as case studies for our investigation. In their view, only a few community-wide examples of such sites existed. And while most of these experts were partially aware of what was happening in their nearby communities, few of them knew what was happening across multiple communities.

Based on these experts' recommendations and our independent search of the literature and Internet, we investigated a number of sites reputed to have relatively strong arts education initiatives involving coordination efforts across multiple organizations. After conducting telephone interviews with the leaders of these sites and analyzing documents, we selected six sites for a more in-depth investigation: Alameda County, California; Boston, Massachusetts; Chicago, Illinois; Dallas, Texas; Los Angeles County, California; and New York City, New York. These six appeared to be among the sites furthest along in their coordinated efforts to improve access to quality arts learning experiences for children in their regions. In addition, they represent diversity in both focus and the genesis of their efforts.

From fall 2006 through spring 2007, we collected documents, conducted phone interviews, and made visits to the sites to gather information on the coordination efforts in these six communities. The site visits included both in-person interviews and some opportunistic classroom observations. During this phase, we interviewed approximately 120 local experts in about 20 interviews per site. These experts represented an array of organizations: state and local government agencies and school districts, foundations, not-for-profit providers, universities, etc. We assembled our interview notes and other materials related to the study sites and then summarized our findings by specific variables. With this information, we identified the case-specific and cross-site themes that make up the main findings of our study.

Important Concepts

Underlying our study is the notion that arts learning can be improved through greater access, more-equitable access, better-quality provision, or more-efficient provision. While our purpose was not to determine the truth of this notion, we did need an idea of what high-quality arts learning might be. In addition, we needed to have an idea of what coordinated, or collaborative, efforts for improvement might look like.

High-Quality Arts Learning

Our literature review and early interviews with experts made it very clear that the arts struggle for a legitimate role in America's education system, both in the formal K–12 public schools and in the more informal, out-of-school-time (OST) forms of provision. The arts have been historically positioned as inherently different from and often ancillary to other school subjects (Wakeford, 2004); they appear to be a subject whose inclusion requires a fight. Supporters of other uses of children's time question the purpose of arts education, what it should look like, and how it should be provided.

It is important to note that the field of arts learning by no means lacks answers to these questions. As much as any other field of learning, it is rich in conceptual complexity. In fact, it may have too many answers claiming different purposes—for example, to teach mastery of an art form, to cultivate understanding and appreciation of the art field, to improve outcomes in other subjects, to develop various life skills. These multiple purposes have combined with shifts in the policy environment to create contrasting approaches to delivery—from in-school, sequential courses, to integration with the rest of the curriculum, to OST provision.

These contrasting views of goals and provision are discussed in more depth in Chapter Two as part of the current ecology of arts education. More generally, we can say that for this study, we accepted arts learning as being of benefit to a child's education. In addition, we assumed that the purposes and goals of arts education are viewed in multiple ways within the arts education community and even within a single organization. As a result, the perceived quality of a specific provision will reflect the extent to which it attains the specific goals set by the parties involved.[3] We also did not adhere to a specific view of what provision ought to be in our study; we simply note that different views of quality provision are important in the field and that disagreements on this topic played out in the case studies.[4]

Attributes of Coordinated Improvement Efforts

Organizations within the public sector usually decide to coordinate their efforts when they have an important shared goal and individually lack the political power or resources needed to achieve it on their own. In those parts of the public sector characterized by resource constraints, such as public education and the arts, coordinated approaches also hold the promise of increasing the efficiency of provision by reducing duplication and gaps in service. Furthermore, agreement among such organizations on what constitutes quality provision can result in more-consistent provision. These expected benefits from coordinated efforts remain theoretical; the existing literature provides little evidence that such efforts are better than other strategies for improving access to arts learning experiences.

To conduct this study, we needed to understand what a coordinated effort to improve arts education might entail and why coordination might be a viable strategy for effecting improvement. The relevant literature, including organizational research on systems building,[5] social service provision through coordinated delivery systems,[6] and collaboration to promote arts education,[7] agrees on the major attributes of cross-organizational improvement initiatives. The following paragraphs briefly describe these attributes, which we used to guide our interview protocols and which are thus reflected in our findings. The first four pertain to all cross-organizational initiatives; the last pertains solely to such initiatives in the public domain.

As a first step and as a continuing task of inter-organizational coordination, a shared goal aimed at some defined improved performance is created or recognized by all the organizations. This step often occurs in response to a problem being recognized because of an evaluation, new legislation, or media attention. Attempts to find partners that share

---

[3]   A related study by Project Zero, at the Harvard Graduate School of Education, focuses on arts programs reputed to be of high quality.

[4]   These differing views of provision could be empirically tested to determine which form(s) of delivery leads to student outcomes of the highest quality. Such a test has never been done, at least in part because of the number of differing views on the benefits of the arts and the difficulties involved in trying to measure some of the proposed benefits.

[5]   We relied heavily on Banathy and Jenlink's 2004 synthesis of this literature.

[6]   See, for example, Keith, 1993; Stone, 1998; Tushnet, 1993; Mattessich and Monsey, 1992; and Dluhy, 1990.

[7]   See Day et al., 1984; Dreeszen, 2001; Dreeszen, Aprill, and Deasy, 1999; Seidel, Eppel, and Martiniello, 2001; Slavkin and Crespin, 2000; Stevenson and Deasy, 2005.

the cause can start with simple networking and then move to convening different parties and ongoing discussions, often culminating in a formal shared mission statement. Case studies indicate that these initial efforts succeed when they are led by organizations seen as legitimate leaders in the specific community or on the issue, and as fence-menders or having an interest in the greater good. In addition, efforts flourish when personnel are assigned to the mission and provided with the time and resources needed to work with others. Seed money and a leader that is effective (that is, capable, inclusive in style, and stable) are recognized as key to these early and ongoing efforts.

The initial efforts grow through routine and effective communication and coordination among the organizations. Communication is supported by regular meetings among representatives, a coordinating organization to facilitate joint work, and a means for group decisionmaking. Leadership style is key to ensuring that group decisionmaking maintains the overall commitment to the common cause.

A major step forward lies in creating and implementing a joint plan of action that includes policies and supporting infrastructure that mutually reinforce the improvement goal. Creation and implementation of the joint plan are supported by information about the environment, the specific problems, available options, etc. Fundraising and resource redistribution are key components of the effort, and specific coordinating structures or implementation structures may grow out of the planning effort.

Because information is essential to all improvement efforts, the coordination bodies often develop feedback loops or information flows that allow them to assess progress toward goals and effectiveness of coordinated responses in bringing about improvement. An array of activities might flourish: collection and use of data on access to and participation in programs; development and use of assessment tools for understanding learning and for diagnosing and addressing failures; assessments of teachers and teaching artists for use in delivering professional development; development and use of data to understand funding flows and determine where additional resources are needed within the system.

Information about the state of the field and what can be done to improve it is often developed and communicated in a way that ensures the information will flow to the public to attract additional partners and support. Public relations and advocacy campaigns aimed at gaining the support of parents, policymakers, and community leaders by making both the need and the solutions visible may be part of this process.

The challenges to coordinated attempts to build collaborative approaches are numerous (Bodilly et al., 2004); lack of consistent and sustained leadership interest, budget shortfalls, and competition among the coordinating organizations for resources are but a few. In addition, the literature we reviewed and our expert interviews indicated that arts education provision involves unique, perhaps formidable challenges. Chapter Two's description of the recent history of the arts education field provides insight into past and current challenges to improving access to high-quality arts learning experiences.

Report Organization

Chapter Two describes the sector that provides arts education opportunities today, setting it in a historical context so that readers can appreciate the enduring challenges facing current improvement initiatives. Chapter Three discusses the six case studies of coordination initiatives to improve access to arts education. Chapter Four synthesizes the sites' common strategies for improving access to quality arts learning experiences regardless of the extent to which the actors involved were working in a coordinated fashion. Chapter Five discusses specific coordination themes that emerged from the analysis, as well as factors that fostered and impeded coordination, and advantages and drawbacks of participating in coordination efforts. Chapter Six reviews the findings and offers conclusions and guidance for practitioners.

Study Limitations

Our study had three important limitations. First, the six sites we used as case studies are among the nation's largest urban centers, each with a rich cultural nexus of museums, theaters, symphonies, galleries, and producing artists that most likely does not exist in smaller urban and non-urban communities. Hence, if such factors prove important, the ability to generalize our findings to smaller cities and rural areas will be reduced. Second, our study is a descriptive analysis of arts education initiatives, not an evaluation of arts learning efforts. Our purpose was to describe what the site communities were attempting to do and how they were doing it, not to evaluate the quality of the arts learning experiences offered in each site. We provide limited information about whether the sites were progressing toward their goals, in large part because the documentation on progress was very limited. Third, this document is a historical snapshot of efforts through spring 2007 and, as such, does not include changes that have occurred in the six sites since then.

CHAPTER TWO

The Evolving Ecology of Arts Education

This chapter presents a common history of arts education across America's urban centers and sets forth important issues that communities must face as they attempt to improve the provision of arts education. We based this discussion on the literature on arts education learning, the oral histories of arts learning provided by experts we interviewed, and what we discovered during our site visits. This chapter illustrates that the field of arts education is conceptually rich and complex, but that arts education initiatives start from a weak position compared with those in other fields of education. The fact that researchers, practitioners, and advocates do not always present a united front on goals and preferred delivery mechanisms for arts education renders coordination across organizations somewhat challenging.

This chapter is organized both chronologically and thematically. We cover the scarcity and variance in local arts education during the 1970s, the fiscal crises that precipitated a decline in provision of arts education during the 1980s and 1990s, the field's fragmentation over the purpose and delivery of arts education, the connection to other education reforms, the growth in types of organizations providing arts learning, and the current set of arts learning providers and influencers.

Scarcity and Variance in Public Arts Education of the 1970s

In 1977, the Arts, Education, and Americans Panel produced a report titled *Coming to Our Senses: The Significance of the Arts in American Education*. Headed by David Rockefeller and counting among its members a former U.S. commissioner of education, this panel, commonly referred to as the "Rockefeller panel," reviewed the state of arts education across the nation and found serious deficits. Many people considered this report controversial (Chapman, 1978; Smith, 1978), but it nonetheless raised the education community's awareness of the status of arts education.

There is little systematic evidence on the scope and provision of arts learning at the time of the Rockefeller panel report. Although only a few states had standards then, some provided curriculum guidelines or outlines. In 1978, Elliot Eisner concluded that the average amount of time devoted to teaching the arts each week was less than one-half hour (Eisner, 1978, p. 15).

In general, each school district's budget and time constraints determined whether arts education was offered to students. It was widely accepted that inclusion of the arts in the curriculum was a local decision. An itinerant arts specialist often instructed, holding scheduled classes across the district's schools. Alternatively, at the elementary level, a regular classroom teacher may have been the primary provider of arts education.

Private provision of arts education outside of school was available for families that sought it and could afford it. In addition to individual private providers, the main providers outside of school were arts production or presentation organizations, such as museums and theater groups, which we call *cultural organizations*. The primary purpose of these organizations was to produce art, but many had small, ancillary educational functions as well. Large museums offered school trips, and children lucky enough to attend a school that supported performing arts might be treated to a performance once each year. One of our respondents called such opportunities "drive by" arts education, referring to the practice of dropping the children at the museum's door and picking them up a few hours later. The children's experience, not usually connected to their specific academic curriculum, was seen as a field trip to gain exposure to the arts.

In sum, local schools were the main providers, local school boards were the main policymakers, and provision varied substantially. Given this, the Rockefeller panel called on American educators to rethink literacy to include the arts and to consider the arts a basic part of school curriculum. As much as the panel had documented a poor state of affairs, it had also documented the rich and complex concepts behind arts education and its role in building a just society. This clarion call failed to have the desired effect, however, in part because of the fiscal crises that followed its release and disagreements about specific recommendations it had made.

Setback Caused by Fiscal Crises

The sites we studied, along with many other communities across the United States, suffered a series of fiscal crises in the mid-1970s through the 1980s that affected schooling. The arts and arts teachers became easy targets for budget cutting. As an example, in 1975–1976, after a decade of crisis and constant budget cuts, the New York City public schools laid off 15,000 teachers—almost 25 percent of the total number. Teachers in subjects considered "less central" were the first to go. According to the Center for Arts Education (CAE), "By 1991, the last year for which systematic arts data was collected by the Board of Education, two-thirds of the schools had no licensed art or music teachers" (2007, p. 10). Schools were no longer encouraged to hire arts teachers, and arts teachers who remained were transferred to other positions.

The other sites in the study reported a similar phenomenon. Respondents reported that there were massive layoffs of arts teachers as each community reached the height of its specific budget crisis. Passage of California's Proposition 13 in 1978, for example, left many school districts unable to maintain their arts programs.

This was not the full extent of what was claimed by the fiscal crises, however. In cities such as Chicago, cuts were made to school operating hours as well as to teaching slots, reducing the school day from what had normally been about seven hours to just five hours and forty-five minutes.[1] Not only were the arts instructors gone, but so was the time in the school day for anything other than the very basic subjects.

Policy shifts at the national level were echoed by cuts in arts education in states and local districts. The federal government's Arts and Humanities Office was cut in 1981 (Herbert, 2004). In 1983, the National Commission on Excellence in Education's *A Nation At Risk: The Imperative for Educational Reform* further eroded arts education's standing by calling for greater attention to basics to address what it said was the American education system's failure to prepare its children for a demanding future. This call, which galvanized the education sector, did not emphasize the arts in its arguments for extensive reforms to keep the United States internationally competitive.

In the mid-1980s, the National Endowment for the Arts (NEA) conducted a congressionally mandated survey on the state of arts education. The result, *Toward Civilization: A Report on Arts Education* (1988), documented then current thinking: Arts education was considered superfluous to a core curriculum and not supportive of the development of critical thinking skills. *Toward Civilization* also found that arts education was predominantly absent in schools, and that the one consensus in the field of arts education was that there was no consensus on what an arts education curriculum should include.

Development of Alternative Views of Purpose and Provision

During the 1970s and 1980s, arts education researchers, practitioners, and advocates struggled to justify continued inclusion of the arts in the school day. Early work by Harvard University's Project Zero led the way in developing the intellectual concepts of the field.[2] These ideas were meshed with growing research by organizations such as the Arts Education Partnership, which documented the multiple benefits of the arts in

---

[1]   Chicago now has the shortest number of hours in a school day of the 50 largest districts in the country (Walsh, 2007).

[2]   The project's reports are available (as of September 9, 2007) at the Project Zero Web site: http://www.pz.harvard.edu.

young people's lives,[3] and were furthered by advocates/scholars such as Jane Remer and Richard Deasy,[4] who connected arts education to school reform efforts. As the blooming research documenting the benefits of arts education combined with differing views on what the goals of arts education should be, somewhat distinct camps of advocates and philosophies of provision came into being.

Diverse Goals and Approaches to Arts Learning

In one sense, it seems obvious that arts learning should be included in the academic core because, quite simply, parents support the arts as vital to a well-rounded education (Davidson and Michener, 2001; California Arts Council, 2001; Harris, 1996). But according to the literature and the experts we interviewed, there are four, possibly distinct, views of the goals for arts learning, and they tend to be associated with different approaches to provision.[5]

One of these views, which emphasizes the creation of art, sees the goal as mastery of one particular art form, which means learning the language of that art form and gaining competence as a creator, performer, audience member, and critic. This goal requires a studio-based or conservatory-style curriculum that focuses on teaching the production mechanics and techniques of a specific art discipline and takes a child through a sequence of stand-alone arts courses from novice to mastery in producing or performing works of art. Schools for the arts tend to follow this conceptualization; they can be found in many cities as stand-alone schools accessed through audition. The student completing this course of study is able to produce professional-level art and has an appreciation of that art's place in history and the aesthetics of the particular form, but may not be familiar with or have a critical appreciation of other art forms and their historical importance.

Then there is the view that the goal is to build artistic appreciation and outlook, which may include but is not primarily focused on producing art (Greene, 2001; Csikszentmihalyi, 1996; Arts Education Partnership, 2004; Arts Education Partnership et al., 2004; Eisner, 1998; Gardner, 1989; McCarthy et al., 2004). The emphasis here is on refining perception and discrimination; developing imagination, mutual sympathy, and the capacity for wonder and awe; and developing the deep understanding that is critical to all learning.[6] Some advocates for building these capacities support "discipline-based curriculum," a concept developed by the Getty Center for Education

---

[3]   The reports are (as of September 9, 2007) on the Arts Education Partnership Web site: http://www.aep-arts.org.

[4]   Specific works by Remer and Deasy are cited, as appropriate, throughout this document.

[5]   Teitelbaum and Gillis, 2003, and McCarthy et al., 2004, provide good summaries of the research.

[6]   Very recently, this line of reasoning led to arguments that early introduction to the arts through active engagement and participation is critical to ensuring adult appreciation of, participation in, and support of the arts (McCarthy et al., 2004; Bergoni and Smith, 1996).

in the Arts in 1982 to emphasize instruction in art history, art criticism, and aesthetics, as well as arts production (Delacruz and Dunn, 1996). Discipline-based curriculum is separate from other core courses and sequential in nature. The child builds significant understanding and appreciation by the end of the schooling experience. Some leaders, such as Maxine Greene, of Lincoln Center, argue for building an aesthetic worldview. They have formed a national network of institutes dedicated to aesthetic education practice centered on deep exploration and understanding of specific works of art to stimulate perception, cognition, affect, and imagination.

Another view grew out of research whose results show that arts education experiences are related to achievement in other school subjects (McCarthy et al., 2004), although Winner and Hetland (2000) argue that this relationship tends to be weak relative to other, more direct actions to increase achievement in other subjects. Some began arguing that arts education should be included in the lives of young people to improve their general and subject-specific achievement levels (Stevenson and Deasy, 2005; Deasy, 2002; Fiske, 1999; Heath, Soep, and Roach, 1998).[7]

In line with this idea that arts education could improve more-general academic outcomes, some schools began to have teachers integrate arts in non-arts subjects. Proponents of integrated arts instruction argue that student achievement in both an art form and other subjects increases through integration experiences (Arts Education Partnership National Forum, 2002; Deasy, 2002; Consortium of National Arts Educators Associations, 2002). Supporters of integrated approaches argue for the arts as "facilitators of the cognitive learning process" (Rabkin and Redmond, 2004, p. 83). This form of provision has the added benefit of fitting the arts into a school day whose time has become heavily devoted to subjects being tested for accountability reasons.

Others, again backed by new research, have taken the view that arts learning could increase motivation, social development, self-confidence, perseverance, and stress reduction (Chapman, 1982; Deasy, 2002; Heath, Soep, and Roach, 1998; Winner and Cooper, 2000). They argue for providing arts learning opportunities to meet the needs of youth development. Provision with this goal in mind would focus on factors that improve motivation and life skills (engagement, practice, drafting and redrafting, social interaction, etc.), as opposed to mastery of a specific form, and that are associated with integrated curriculum provision as well as discipline-based curriculum.

Growth in Contrasting Approaches to Provision

Given the different views on the goals of arts education, different views on where and by whom arts education should be provided are not a surprise.

---

[7] The fact that advocates for arts education feel they need to justify its inclusion is a clear indication that the arts are treated differently from subjects that some consider more central to a core curriculum. Research on arts education struggles to justify the importance of the arts based on how arts learning contributes to the learning of other subjects, whereas advocates for the inclusion of mathematics, science, and history feel no need to prove that these subjects contribute to arts understanding.

In school and/or outside of school. Support for emphasizing in-school arts education has been based on the idea that all students should have equitable access to the arts and the assumption that districts and schools ensure similar levels of exposure for all students (Chapman, 1982; von Zastrow and Janc, 2004). OST programs are available through an array of suppliers (Sousa, 2004), but sole reliance on this form of provision may not meet equity concerns because access (in terms of cost, transportation, etc.) to these programs varies considerably from child to child (Bodilly and Beckett, 2005). Nevertheless, one expert we interviewed argued that "in-school arts instruction alone is doomed. Children must transfer their interest in art outside the classroom if they are to be truly engaged."

Stand-alone or integrated. Those who see the goal of arts education as performance and creation of artworks tend to favor sequential stand-alone courses as the means of delivery. Integration of arts education with other learning is favored by those who see the goal as support of other types of learning or who do not view performance and creation as essential to the benefits they seek. Integration approaches also are seen as a way to include the arts in a school day that has been allowing less and less time for subjects other than those tested for accountability reasons.[8]

Who teaches. Classroom teachers, arts specialists, and artists can all act as arts education instructors, but which of these groups is "best" is a source of debate within the community (Deasy, 2002). The issue of who teaches the arts has important implications for professional development, which is a critical need in the field (Longley, 1999). The debate centers on questions about whether pedagogical or artistic skills are more important in teaching the arts.

Connections to and Effect of Other Education Reform Efforts

Since the fiscal crises of the 1970s and 1980s, major changes in the education reform landscape and in education reform policy have affected arts education: the introduction of standards across the curriculum, the development and growth of test-based accountability, the introduction of site-based management, and more-general school reform efforts. Each has had a different impact on the arts education ecology.

Development of Arts Goals and Standards

The state-level movement to develop curriculum standards took place in the 1980s and 1990s and gained momentum in the 1990s from the federal push for national education goals and standards. With support from the NEA and the Getty Center for Education in the Arts, the professional associations of teachers of music, dance, the-

---

[8] It is no coincidence that schools turned to integrated arts approaches as time in the school day began dwindling for subjects outside the accountability realm.

ater, and visual arts developed national content standards that were issued in 1994 as the National Standards for Arts Education. Despite the existence of these national arts standards, however, the arts were not in the national goals set forth in the proposed NCLB federal legislation. Only through efforts led by the Kennedy Center, the NEA, and the Getty Center for Education in the Arts were the arts included as a national education goal in this major piece of federal legislation.

All of these federal standards for subjects are voluntary; there is no enforcement mechanism. Since 1994, almost every state has adopted some form of content standards for arts education, and some states also include guidelines for time per week to be devoted to arts education. However, because implementation of these standards and guidelines is left to districts and schools—many of which are pressed for school time and space, and all of which are held accountable for subjects other than the arts—claims to have met requirements tend to be based on very broad interpretations of the standards and guidelines.

Growth of High-Stakes Accountability and Assessments

Another part of the struggle for arts legitimacy in the curriculum concerns how to assess student learning in the arts. Researchers, practitioners, and advocates have long argued about whether and how to develop quality indicators and valid, transparent, and reliable assessments. As late as 1988, the NEA was still laying out the pros and cons of whether to develop assessments at all (NEA, 1988), coming down firmly for the development of tests in the arts, partly to enable curriculum and pedagogical improvement and partly to ensure the field's legitimacy. In 1992, the Arts Education Consensus Project, sponsored by the National Assessment Governing Board, began an 18-month effort to establish objectives for an arts test to be administered as part of the National Assessment of Educational Progress (NAEP).[9] The resulting, voluntary test covered visual arts, music, and theater. Although it was administered in 1994 and then never used again by the federal or any state government (National Center for Education Statistics [NCES], 1998), it represents an important step forward in the development of valid and reliable tests for the arts.

Since then, Kentucky, Oklahoma, Washington, New Jersey, and Maryland have made efforts to assess arts learning. About 12 states, including the five just named, provide sample assessment items, professional development, and other supports, but only Kentucky includes arts in its mandated state-level student achievement tests. In other words, despite decades of efforts, arts assessment in most of the United States consists of individual teachers developing and using their own assessments to suit their own needs.

One implication of this situation is that supporters of specific improvement efforts do not have the quality assessment tools needed to prove the effectiveness of those

---

[9]   An NAEP administration 20 years earlier had included music and visual arts.

improvements. They might be able to show a connection between their arts education programs and test scores for subjects other than the arts, but there is no way for them to demonstrate more-direct learning and achievement via reliable and valid measures.

The most recent federal survey of arts provision (1999–2000) occurred before the advent of strong standards-based reform in most states. It showed that music and visual arts instruction were available in some form in, respectively, 94 percent and 87 percent of U.S. elementary schools (NCES, 2002a). A closer look at the data revealed that across all schools, students received an average of 72 minutes per week of music and about 60 minutes per week of visual arts. Fewer than 20 percent of elementary schools offered dance or theater, however. Similarly, most secondary schools offered some music and visual arts: 90 percent and 93 percent, respectively. Of secondary schools, 57 percent offered four or fewer courses in music and 62 percent offered four or fewer courses in visual arts; 48 percent had theater/drama and 14 percent had dance.

More-recent studies show a declining presence of the arts in public schools. Despite the arts' position as a core subject in the national education goals and in NCLB legislation, their place in school curriculum is being eroded by NCLB's requirements for and focus on reading and mathematics. Recent studies demonstrate declines in the time set aside for the arts. Instructional time is increasingly dedicated to "teaching to" the standardized tests, and non-tested subjects, such as the arts and foreign languages, are most at risk for marginalization (Rowe et al., 2004; Hamilton et al., 2007; McMurrer, 2007; Woodworth, Gallagher, and Guha, 2007; West, 2007). More-specific information on this situation is not easy to obtain because of data issues.[10]

Some states have documented dramatic reductions in arts education in the past 20 years.[11] One-quarter of public school principals surveyed in Illinois, Maryland, New Mexico, and New York reported decreases in instructional time for the arts, and the proportion of principals reporting such decreases in high-minority schools, at 36 percent, was even greater (von Zastrow and Janc, 2004). According to a report on music in California public schools, the proportion of students taking music classes fell from 18.5 percent in 1999 to 9.3 percent in 2004—a 50 percent decline. In the same period, the number of music teachers in the state declined by nearly 27 percent, representing an actual loss of 1,053 teachers (Music for All Foundation, 2004). Teachers left in the schools are reportedly struggling to maintain a focus on the arts (Oreck, 2004).

---

[10] The NCES did small-scale surveys in academic years 1995 and 1999, and an Arts Report Card survey in 1997. Given their limited sampling size, these surveys provide only a glimpse of the state of affairs for arts education. Some of the data that are available—unfortunately, not for all locales—are number of arts instructors, course offerings, and available resources (e.g., classroom space, supplies, and funds).

[11] State-level surveys have been completed in Illinois, Kentucky, Rhode Island, and Washington (Ruppert and Nelson, 2006); California (Music for All Foundation, 2004); and Ohio (Ohio Arts Council, 2001). One of the most recent efforts is the New Jersey Arts Education Census Project, conducted in April 2006, which aims to understand the levels of access, equity, and quality for teachers and students in New Jersey schools.

The marginalization of arts education within schools may be associated with the decline in the number of arts specialists retained in districts. In von Zastrow and Janc's study of four states, the number of arts specialists decreased in 23 percent of high-minority schools and 14 percent of low-minority schools, and only 9 percent of both types of schools reported an increase in the number of arts specialists (2004, p. 16). Media reports also reveal declines (Associated Press, 2005; Mezzacappa, 2006). These reports suggest two reasons for decreases in the number of arts teachers: Schools have limited capabilities for hiring and retaining teachers (Southern Regional Education Board, 2002), and arts specialists are in limited supply in some areas (Guthrie and Hamlin, 2002).

Decentralization and the Principal's Role in Curriculum Decisions

Communities have taken different routes in grappling with mandatory high-stakes accountability. In some communities, the central school district office mandates specific curriculum and instruction and has removed curriculum discretion from the schools. Other communities have moved in the direction of decentralization, more commonly known as site-based management. These communities give principals authority over curriculum and instruction in exchange for meeting established goals. Several cities and counties we visited had undertaken site-based management reforms in concert with the standards-based reforms discussed above.

The coupling of test-based accountability that focuses primarily on reading and mathematics scores with site-based management has sometimes had a negative impact on arts education. For example, the Chicago Public Schools adopted a specific form of site-based management that left many decisions about curriculum and instruction to school principals and their local school councils. Principals were primarily held accountable for reading and mathematics test scores. Faced with a shortened school day and school year and detailed accountability criteria, they had to decide where to focus attention. It should not be surprising that most principals reportedly chose to focus on reading and mathematics, to the detriment of the arts.

District officials in three of our case-study sites that moved to site-based management (Chicago, Boston, and New York City) reported that despite state regulations, public schools varied significantly on whether to provide arts programming. Nevertheless, respondents reported that at least some principals remained convinced of the effectiveness of including the arts in the school curriculum. Both arts directors within the districts and community-based providers reported that they were working principal by principal, school by school to create partnerships to maintain or revive arts programs under these conditions.

Even sites with a lesser degree of site-based management reported that the principal was playing a key role in determining the focus of instruction in his or her school. The principal was signaling to teachers the level and type of instruction to provide in the face of competing demands for limited time, space, and funding. As more principals are held accountable for mathematics and language test scores, more of them may be inclined to emphasize these two subjects over other subjects (Hamilton et al., 2007; McMurrer, 2007).

The Arts as the Reform

In the late 1980s, arguments for systemic reforms to improve schools increasingly surfaced (Smith and O'Day, 1990). Using the growing evidence of arts education's contribution to student achievement and to motivation and perseverance, arts advocates began connecting arts education with systemic reform movements. Their argument was that infusion of the arts into the curriculum could serve as the focus of curriculum and pedagogical improvement designed to engage students in learning.

Two major and well-funded efforts to redesign schools supported this idea: the Annenberg Challenge Grants and the New American Schools Corporation design competition. A third effort, by the Galef Institute, developed an arts-rich design for schools called Different Ways of Knowing. Each effort produced significant demonstrations of how the arts could be integrated throughout the curriculum, but they all then foundered through lack of further funding for expansion to more schools. Nevertheless, some people in the field who are closely linked with arts integration advocates (Rabkin and Redmond, 2004; Burnaford, Aprill, and Weiss, 2001; Remer, 1990, 1996) still support such approaches, and some funders, such as The Ford Foundation, are supporting more demonstrations.

Organizational Ecology of Arts Education Today

Our review of themes in the development of the arts education field made it clear to us that the players have changed and grown in number since the early 1970s, when the stage belonged largely to local school districts, schools, and a few cultural organizations. An array of arts learning providers has entered the field in response to changes in fiscal support for arts education, and more government agencies and philanthropic organizations now take part.

Figure 2.1 summarizes the current organizational ecology of arts education. The *providers* shown are the entities that furnish arts learning experiences to children; the *influencers* are the policy and funding entities that furnish rules, regulations, oversight, funding, and goals to the providers. Information on the availability and quality of arts education resources supported by the different entities shown in the figure is diffuse and specific to each state and community.

Non-School Providers

During the past several decades of declining provision of arts education in the schools, three types of non-school providers of arts learning experiences have emerged:

Figure 2.1
Providers and Influencers of K–12 Arts Learning Experiences Within Communities

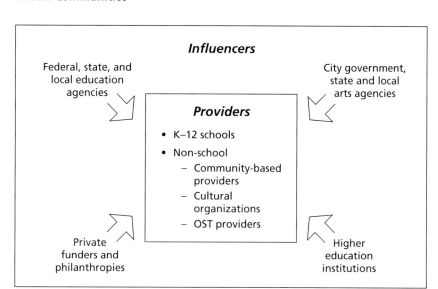

RAND *MG702-2.1*

community-based providers, cultural organizations, and OST providers. In contrast to arts education provision in the early 1970s, today's arts learning opportunities are thus much more likely to come from a more diverse set of providers, although there are no hard data showing the relative contributions of the groups. We discuss each non-school provider and its specific role in turn.

Community-based providers. We call any organization that sprang from the community specifically to improve arts education a *community-based provider*. These organizations originally served a brokering function for schools interested in adopting integrated curriculum or having artists teach courses for their students. They recruited and trained a pool of qualified artist educators who could fill slots for school courses (e.g., a practicing painter for a visual arts course in a school)[12] or could work with general educators to integrate arts into a specific curriculum.

Some community-based providers have expanded their functions to include professional development of artists on standards and pedagogy, professional development of teachers in arts concepts for their subjects, internships for students, artist residencies for schools, etc. Regardless of the specific functions provided, however, all organizations that we included in this category help connect artist educators with schools, OST programs, and cultural organizations so that they can teach the arts through courses and performances with educational workshops.

---

[12] This practice is rare in some of the states that require a certified teacher in each classroom.

As an example, ArtsConnection was founded in New York City in 1979 as a not-for-profit organization whose goal was to connect professional artists with students and teachers in school-based programs. Funded through both the city and its own fundraising efforts, ArtsConnection identified professional artists and matched them to schools to deliver school-specific arts learning programs. In addition, it provided professional development in curriculum development and pedagogy for artists.

Other non-profit community-based providers, each with its own niche and varying functions, sprang up in New York City during this period, including such nationally known organizations as Studio in a School and Education Through Music. Organizations were created in other cities as well, either to match professional artists with schools or to train artists to be teaching artists. Urban Gateways (founded in the early 1960s) and the Chicago Arts Partnerships in Education (CAPE, founded in 1993) are similar organizations with national reputations for partnering with schools to provide arts experiences during the school day. Additionally, Young Audiences and other such organizations emerged to enable children to experience live performances in their own communities.

These types of organizations often receive significant funding from public sources, such as state or city cultural agencies, and from foundations and other corporate and individual donors. This subsidization is what makes these arts learning opportunities affordable for some schools that otherwise could not offer arts education to their students. Many schools accessing these services use limited discretionary funds to pay nominal fees to cover the remaining cost.

The emergence of community-based providers has been beneficial on several fronts. Students receive arts learning, although the level of their exposure to it varies from school to school and grade to grade; artists receive a steady stipend for their work, supplementing their often erratic pay; teachers learn how to use the arts in their curricula; and schools receive services without having to pay full cost.

Cultural organizations. Cultural organizations responded to the arts education void resulting from school budget cuts by increasing their education functions. Our interviewees disclosed that the governing bodies of cultural organizations in each city considered the implications of budget cuts for arts education and decided to respond by increasing their education programming, partly to ensure the organizations would have future supporters. As they redirected funds into education programs, these organizations began to develop closer ties to school districts and schools. Their education programming can include but is not limited to tours of exhibits geared to children's ages and courses of study; lesson plans for teachers that are specifically aligned with state curriculum standards or course requirements; online curriculum that includes tours of their works for distance learning settings; professional development for teachers and artists; networking opportunities for those interested in arts education; family-friendly activities to encourage parents and children to become aware of and experience the arts.

A few cultural organizations have gone even further. For example, the Lincoln Center Institute for the Arts in Education was formed to support aesthetic education throughout the New York City region through partnerships with schools that engage artist educators and reconfigure curriculum and instruction to promote aesthetic capacity. The institute also offers an array of other supports, including professional development and consulting. It and others often team with magnet schools for the arts or help support charter schools that have strong arts components.

This response from the cultural organizations, like that of the community-based providers, has benefited many parties. Students can access arts experiences (often closely aligned with their other academic experiences), and cultural organizations can gain support in their communities from parents and from students—the potential future arts consumers and supporters of these organizations.

Out-of-school-time providers. Another trend during this period was the entry of mothers into the workforce and the resulting growth in OST care provision. According to the U.S. Census Bureau, in 1970, 21 percent of women with children under age 18 worked. By 2002, this proportion had grown to 73 percent, putting the number of children under age 18 whose mothers worked at 67.4 million, and causing both private and public providers of OST programs to grow in number and flourish.

Some, but certainly not all, of these providers offer arts learning as part of their programming. For example, some Boys and Girls Clubs and YMCAs and YWCAs offer arts learning. So do city-run departments of parks and recreation, and schools in before- and after-school care programs. In many cases, community-based providers (described above) fill the need for arts instructors in these types of programs.

OST provision does not reach all children, however. Estimates of unmet demand vary widely, some indicating that as many as two-thirds of children who may need such services cannot or do not access them (Bodilly and Beckett, 2005). Many families cannot afford or do not have easy access to OST providers. It remains a voluntary endeavor, which means that not all children receive it. And children who do receive it do not always receive arts education, much less high-quality arts experiences.

Influencers

Many different entities influence arts education: the federal government and state governments, school district offices, foundations, colleges and universities, and state and local arts agencies. Some of these were included in the discussion of providers, above; here we cover the major groups of influencers and specify their slightly different roles as influencers in arts learning.

City government and state and local arts agencies. These entities support arts education by funding programming, often with federal, state, and local dollars. City government agencies play myriad roles that influence arts learning. For example, cities support museums and theaters by providing public space and grants for programming, and children then take advantage of productions offered. City agencies overlap with

OST providers at times—for example, when city parks and recreation departments provide arts programming after school and during the summer. City departments of cultural affairs, funded by state and local tax dollars, support arts education in our case-study sites, underwriting non-school education programs for students talented in specific ways and providing infrastructure (vetted lists of arts specialists who can be called on for teaching) to support other programs. State arts agencies often work through competitive grants, and local arts education programs apply for funding to support their work. In short, these agencies strive to provide the arts production function in localities and access to the arts, and they even support specific learning venues.

Private funders and philanthropies. Community-based providers and cultural organizations rely in part on local and national philanthropies to underwrite their efforts. Local foundations reported to us that they began in the 1970s and 1980s to significantly reallocate funding to such local organizations to ensure that children received some arts education. Indeed, local foundations are major funders of arts education in each of our six case-study sites. But not all foundations are simply behind-the-scenes funders. As discussed above, philanthropic organizations—the Annenberg Foundation, the Getty Center for Education in the Arts, The Ford Foundation, The William and Flora Hewlett Foundation, The Wallace Foundation, etc.—have assumed major, national roles in the provision of arts learning through various contributions, including development of discipline-based constructs, development of national standards and the arts NAEP assessment, and support for arts infusion demonstrations.

Federal, state, and local education agencies. Even though states are not bound by the national standards and the inclusion of the arts in core curriculum, both of these were huge steps forward in supporting efforts to build consensus on what should be taught in schools. State public education agencies provide funding for local schools, as well as specific standards, curriculum and instructional guides, and some professional development supports for these schools. As such, these agencies influence but do not control the types and levels of arts education provided in schools and in after-school programs on school premises. Many states mandate arts education provision, but the absence of funding and accountability means that school districts and schools can and do interpret the mandates to suit their local circumstances.

Higher education institutions. Because schools of higher education train and provide the teachers and artists who interact directly with children, they are responsible for developing the arts specialist and artist educator pipelines into the schools and programs. Higher education institutions are in a position to heavily influence the quality of arts learning through the teachers and teaching artists themselves and their preparation. In addition, these institutions affect the supply of teachers and artists in a very unregulated market.

Interactions Among Providers and Influencers

Outside of normal contractual relationships (such as the school district central office contracting with providers for specific services), the main types of providers and influencers discussed above usually do not act in a coordinated fashion within communities to support arts learning. In fact, the opposite is more likely to be true. A previous discussion pointed to the negative effects of test-based accountability on the arts in schools and to the detrimental impact that the combination of test-based accountability, budget cuts, and site-based management has had on arts education in some schools. Some influencers, such as philanthropies, have acted to counter these negative trends in arts education, but seldom have they coordinated their actions. For example, philanthropies differ in their preferences for integrated versus discipline-based programs and for specific arts or arts experiences. In the absence of coordinated actions, these differences strongly affect what arts opportunities are presented to different children across a city and which arts education providers thrive or languish.

The experts we interviewed all agreed that the combination in communities of layers of regulations, different influences, and stovepiped funding streams has created a checkerboard effect. Each community has some outstanding arts opportunities; but for the majority of children, the array of arts offerings—if offerings exist for them at all—is idiosyncratic and unreliable. Children's arts opportunities are shaped by such factors as specific school attended, access to transportation, and funding for OST programs. Respondents in each community noted that fine magnet school arts programs were in place for selected students, but that the majority of students faced a confused array of arts offerings that often changed from one year to the next as influencers changed funding support or policies.

Summary

This chapter has demonstrated that arts education in the public sphere struggles for legitimacy and for time and space in the school day. Arts education is characterized by a diverse array of providers, some of them competing with each other for the attention of children and families, and all of them competing with school subjects that have the benefit of greater attention and greater resources. Progress has been made through such steps as setting national standards, creating a national assessment, and producing research that supports arts benefits. But factors such as high-stakes testing and fiscal constraints have placed limits on progress. In short, most public provision of arts learning faces a constant struggle for space, time, and resources. Furthermore, the policymakers and funders with the most influence over the provision of arts education are a diverse group unaccustomed to working in coordination with each other.

In this situation, coordinated efforts among providers and influencers of arts education would seem to be the most natural way to jointly overcome the challenges.

But the effort to find a common cause is stymied by extensive disagreement in the field about goals and appropriate approaches for arts education. And matters are not improved by the severe fiscal conditions that exist in the arts education field, conditions that can promote competition where coordination is sorely needed. The next chapters investigate how these themes played out in the sites we studied.

CHAPTER THREE

Coordination Efforts Within Six Communities

This chapter describes the coordination efforts undertaken in our six case-study sites, or communities, to improve arts learning. Our intent here is to set the stage for the findings of our cross-site analyses, which are discussed in Chapters Four and Five. We thus provide only the information needed to discern the efforts' differences and similarities, without regard to the quality of the arts learning provided.

The six communities had much in common when they began their efforts. All had very vibrant arts sectors comprising theaters, symphonies, museums, etc. All had a varied set of arts education providers, as well as foundations and state agencies that promoted arts learning. In short, all six communities had a strong set of arts assets from which to build a collaboration.

Furthermore, each community was within a state that had established school-curriculum content standards for the arts, mandates on the time schools were to spend per year on arts courses, and certification requirements for arts teachers.[1] Table 3.1 sets out the relevant characteristics of the six school systems. As shown, schools in these communities were serving mainly minority students, many of whom were eligible for free or reduced-price lunches (an indicator of poverty). Many of the schools were also considered low performing. Each school district or set of school districts had experienced budget cuts over the years that affected the provision of school-based arts education. And the current accountability requirements and school-based management had eroded support for arts education in many schools and led to uneven access to arts education across schools.

Despite these commonalities, the arts education coordination efforts in these communities varied considerably, partially because of context and circumstances and partially because of choices each site made on important issues: location of provision (in school, OST), type of teacher (classroom teacher, arts teacher, teaching artist), form of delivery (stand-alone, integrated), groups to involve as partners, and who would lead the effort. Table 3.2 lists the choices made per site within the context of the collaborative initiative we chose to focus on in our study.

---

[1] Education Commission of the States, 2005, lists state policies on arts education.

Table 3.1
Characteristics of the Six Case-Study Sites

Characteristic	Alameda County	Boston[a]	Chicago[b]	Dallas[c]	Los Angeles County	New York City
Total population[d]	1,500,000	559,000	2,800,000	1,200,000	9,900,000	8,100,000
Number of districts	18	1	1	1	80	32[e]
Total enrollment in public school district(s)	213,500[f]	57,000[f]	421,000	160,000[f]	1,700,000[f]	1,100,000[f]
Number of schools	350	145	623	225	1,700	1,200
Student demographics						
Percent white	25	14	8	5	19	11
Percent black	17	42	49	30	11	27
Percent Hispanic, any race	28	34	38	64	59	50
Percent eligible for free and reduced-price lunch	32[g]	71	86	71[h]	64	72[h]
Percentage of schools meeting federal adequate yearly progress standards in 2006	60	n/a	41.2	72	71	69[i]

[a] All column data are 2006–07 from at-a-glance section of Boston Public Schools Web site (Boston Public Schools, undated) unless noted otherwise.

[b] All column data are FY2005–06 from at-a-glance section of Chicago Public Schools Web site (Chicago Public Schools, undated), unless noted otherwise.

[c] Dallas Independent School District.

[d] Based on 2005 or 2006 U.S. Census data estimates.

[e] This is the number of districts that New York City had when the case study began. By the end of the study, it had restructured as site-based management of all schools under one district.

[f] Based on 2007–08 data.

[g] As of 2001–02 (California Food Policy Advocates, 2002).

[h] As of 2001–02 (NCES, 2002b, Part 2 of Table 9).

[i] New York State Board of Regents, 2007.

The following sections describe the six communities in alphabetical order as of our study period. For each site, we offer information on context and motivation for change, coordination goals and efforts, and achievements as well as some prospects for the future.

Alameda County

In Alameda County, California, which is home to the cities of Berkeley and Oakland in the East Bay area, we focused on the countywide effort known as Alliance for Arts Learning Leadership. This effort had been in existence for over eight years at the time of our interviews (December 2006) and involved school districts, schools, cultural insti-

Table 3.2
Key Choices of the Six Collaborative Efforts

Collaborative Effort	Leadership	Partners	Location of Provision	Form of Delivery	Type of Teacher
Alameda County: Alliance for Arts Learning Leadership	County Department of Education	Broad spectrum of providers and influencers	In school	Primarily integration	Teaching artist, teacher, arts teacher
Boston: Arts in OST improvement efforts	No clear lead	Mayor's office, BASB[a], foundations, community providers, cultural organizations	OST	Not specified	Teaching artist
Chicago: Establishing an arts education advocate position in the school district	Local foundation coalition and district head-quarters	School district, foundations	In school	Stand-alone courses	Arts teacher
Dallas: Big Thought (Young Audiences through DALI[b])	Community-based organization	Full spectrum of providers and influencers	In school, OST	Integration, stand-alone courses, neighborhood offerings	Teaching artist, teacher, arts teacher
Los Angeles County: Arts for All	County Arts Commission	Broad spectrum of providers and influencers	In school	Integration, stand-alone courses	Teaching artist, teacher, arts teacher
New York City: Step-Up initiative	District headquarters	School districts, foundations, other city agencies	In school	Stand-alone courses	Teaching artist, arts teacher

[a] Boston After School and Beyond.
[b] Dallas Arts Learning Initiative.

tutions, community-based providers, parents, businesses, and higher education institutions. Similar to the situation in Los Angeles County (described below), the effort was being led by a county public-sector organization external to the school districts.

Context and Motivation for Change

In Alameda County, with its 18 different school districts, arts education was slowly dismantled as the effects of Proposition 13, passed by California's voters in 1978, reduced funding for local school districts. Provision of arts learning in the schools came to be uneven across the county. In California, the individual school districts provide education while the county offices of education provide mandated and voluntary services to the districts, such as review of district budgets, registration of teacher credentials, and professional development. In 1999, the newly elected Superintendent of Schools for Alameda County was dissatisfied with the provision of arts learning across the county and took action to improve it.

The superintendent clearly articulated her motivation for the effort: to systematically improve arts learning based on the belief that each child deserves a well-rounded, high-quality education, and that learning in and through the arts creates equitable classrooms and develops well-functioning adults. She saw unequal provision across school districts as a social justice issue. In addition, she was looking for a systematic approach, not piecemeal funding to aid isolated programs.

Coordination Goals and Efforts

The superintendent created an Arts Learning Manager position and hired a local, former arts-magnet school teacher for the position. Forty percent of the manager's salary came from the county; the rest was covered by grant funding. The manager's assignment was to systemically improve arts learning throughout the county. Soon after her hire, the county received a small state grant to implement standards-based instruction in music, dance, drama, and visual arts. Instead of simply passing this funding on to specific programs, the superintendent and arts manager used it to initiate systemic change. The arts learning manager convened countywide conversations, gathering together key arts education leaders who first came to exchange ideas and eventually served on advisory boards for the county's work. She used the $25,000 grant to involve five districts and their communities in a strategic planning process and helped them garner ongoing resources to support their plans. In 2001, the Alliance for Arts Learning Leadership was born of these efforts, so named to convey the belief that strong, sustainable leadership for this work must be cultivated across communities and at every level of the education system.

The goal of the Alliance for Arts Learning Leadership was for every student in every school in the county to have access to arts education every day.[2] The alliance supported both teaching the arts as a stand-alone discipline and integrating the arts into other subjects to enhance learning in both the arts and other disciplines. Its leadership believed that arts integration is necessary to link arts learning to a high-quality education for every child every day in a well-rounded education in all content areas.

The Alliance for Arts Learning Leadership grew to be a network of individuals and organizations that included K–12 arts specialists, community-based providers, cultural organization representatives, artists, classroom teachers, school district officials, postsecondary education representatives, and members of school reform and parent organizations. Overseen by a 25-member steering committee and an advisory group made up of district arts education leaders, it held regular meetings, engaged in strategic planning, and established both informal feedback mechanisms, primarily through its relationship with its advisory group, and formal feedback mechanisms, via external evaluations of its work.

---

2   For full details on the Alliance for Arts Learning Leadership, see http://www.artiseducation.org/aall/aall.htm.

The Alliance for Arts Learning Leadership received funding from The Ford Foundation to support its strategic planning sessions. It also relied on grants from the federal government and county funding. The state arts council provided some grants, and local businesses and others sponsored the alliance's annual art shows of students' work.

The overarching strategy of the Alliance for Arts Learning Leadership was to develop arts education leaders at multiple levels. It offered services and funding to attract school districts and schools to join and then built the capacity of individual artists, teachers, principals, and district administrators to provide arts education in these districts and schools. In this way, the alliance hoped to create distributed leadership to sustain programs in the case of staff turnover, funding fluctuations, and even the disappearance of the alliance itself.

The activities of the Alliance for Arts Learning Leadership included

- *Supporting Model Arts Programming (MAP) districts.* The Alliance for Arts Learning Leadership worked with districts to assess current arts programs and strategically plan for equitable access to the arts using a district assessment tool kit, training on assessment and planning, professional development, funding, and technical assistance. It mentored district leaders and community members and ensured sharing through quarterly meetings for MAP district leaders. School and school district plans varied; the alliance did not promote a particular model.
- *Supporting arts anchor schools.* Arts anchor schools operating in Berkeley, Emeryville, and Oakland school districts developed an arts education plan that was regularly reviewed by district-based facilitators. The Alliance for Arts Learning Leadership established a network of arts providers, school reform coaches, and teaching artists to support anchor schools and their districts. This network met monthly to share and build better practices. The alliance also coordinated arts learning seminars for all arts learning anchor sites three times a year.
- *Developing a professional community.* The Alliance for Arts Learning Leadership facilitated exchanges of information and resources by providing professional development to school-level teams to develop curriculum and conduct action research. Local arts college officials were active in providing professional development through and with the alliance.
- *Building advocacy.* The Alliance for Arts Learning Leadership developed leaders at multiple levels in support of a countywide advocacy campaign to expand visibility of and support for arts education. It was training students, parents, teachers, principals, and district officials to speak with one voice so that they would more clearly articulate why arts learning matters to the education of the whole child, strong schools, and healthy communities. Alliance members had recently formed an "Arts Active Parents" group to advocate for arts education for their children. The alliance also supported regular arts exhibits showcasing student artwork and testimonials on the impact of arts education.

- *Improving quality of instruction.* The Alliance for Arts Learning Leadership promoted quality by infusing the state's visual and performing arts standards throughout all of its professional development sessions and its support for schools and school districts. It was training local artists and arts organizations in how to use state standards and training community-based providers and coaches who then could provide support and training throughout the county. This cascading training model promoted a standard of quality among community-based providers and coaches.

Achievements to Date and Future Prospects

The Alliance for Arts Learning Leadership has helped build stable leadership, attract new resources, and create a network of organizations and individuals working in coordinated fashion to improve access to high-quality arts learning experiences. Members credited their lobbying efforts for the new state funding for arts education. Local community-based providers credited the alliance with increasing their opportunities to successfully win new grants. After eight years, 13 of Alameda County's 18 school districts were involved in the alliance, developing or implementing a plan to serve all students in their districts.

With new funds from the state, the alliance was planning to expand its work— and herein lay a new challenge. The alliance would have to develop mechanisms to encourage the participation of school districts and schools that so far had not been interested in arts education. There was no way to know whether the new state funding would provide a sufficient incentive for districts and schools to improve their arts offerings. Moreover, community-based providers in Alameda County expressed concern that if demand did indeed grow, they might not be able to increase their current level of services. The county simply might not have enough artists and arts organizations to respond to growing demand for support and capacity building.

Boston

In Boston, we were pointed toward the OST community's efforts to improve access to OST activities, which included support from foundations and the mayor's office to improve access to arts learning activities in particular. At the time of our interviews (April 2007), the endeavors aimed at including arts learning in the OST sector were nascent and were headed by leaders from multiple organizations; there was no single, strong collaborative effort.

Context and Motivation for Change

Boston Public Schools was governed by a board appointed by the mayor, and school principals had been given considerable say over curriculum and instruction in return for meeting specified standards for student achievement. Schools were given an allotment (based on student enrollment) for teachers of special subjects, such as arts and physical education. Some schools spent this allotment on science teachers, others on special education teachers, others on arts teachers.

In 1995, a staff position for Curriculum and Instruction, Fine Arts, was created to implement a newly developed arts policy. This office developed arts standards in dance, music, theater, and visual arts in 1997 and provided course descriptions in 1999. In 2003, the Curriculum and Instruction, Fine Arts, staff began bringing in a series of grants to support modest expansion. At the time of our study, the office was providing support to schools to improve the arts.

Interviewees argued that despite these efforts internal to the school system, school autonomy combined with continued budget constraints and high-stakes accountability had led to what was seen as a random set of arts opportunities in the public schools. Some schools had become very supportive of arts learning; others were less so as they sought to increase test scores in mathematics and reading.

In this context, groups in the community, including the mayor's office, foundations, philanthropists, and community-based organizations, had begun to look elsewhere for ways to improve arts provision, focusing on the growing OST initiatives. The different actors all described their goal for OST overall as working to provide equal opportunities for all children, with a heavy focus on at-risk youth in poorly served neighborhoods and reducing incidences of violence and other negative youth behavior. Several foundations also saw support for OST programs as a way to expose youth to the arts as a creative endeavor, thereby enriching their lives and, it was hoped, sparking the motivation to continue in school and avoid risky behaviors.

Coordination Goals and Efforts

Boston was clearly a center of OST activity, but the extent of coordination among the various parties was somewhat unclear. We describe the arrangement in Boston at the time of our study as one of many partners with no more than nascent coordination among them, especially as concerns the arts.

Early efforts by the Boston-based foundations—the Barr Foundation, Boston Foundation, and Cloud Foundation—focused the OST initiative on arts learning by funding research and audits of arts provision. From 1990 to about 2000, these foundations funded efforts to establish a community-based organization, Arts in Progress, to advocate for arts education and provide a broker-like service to ensure that school and OST programs accessed quality providers of arts learning, as well as quality curriculum and materials. Arts in Progress was led by a longtime community advocate for the arts who was credited both with bringing diverse groups together to plan and with having a style that alienated partners essential to the success of the efforts. This collaborative initiative has been credited with some successes, such as influencing the development of the 1994 Boston Public Schools arts policy. Its efforts fell apart when the director left for another position, and it faded from the scene as efforts by the mayor's office and others to provide more-general OST programs began to take hold.

In the late-1990s, the mayor's office announced that all public schools in Boston would remain open until 6 p.m. for after-school programs and began a serious effort, supported by foundations, to improve OST programming. In addition, a community-based initiative led by local philanthropists sprang up to push for greater OST opportunities. In 2004, these two OST coordination efforts merged to form Boston After School and Beyond (BASB), a public/private partnership, to organize the networks and organizations comprising the OST field into a coherent system with the goal of expanding access to high-quality programming (Boston After School and Beyond, undated). This partnership raised over $30 million to support OST provision. The Robert Wood Johnson Foundation sponsored a year-long planning effort for BASB to strengthen provision. With foundation support, audits of OST programs—including some that provided arts learning—were posted to the mayor's office Web site for all to access. Locations of youth violence were mapped and overlapped with maps of OST activity provision to determine useful locations for new programs.

Because the coordination activities just described were not specific to the arts, other individuals and organizations attempted to fill some specifically arts-related gaps. For example, the Mayor's Office of Arts, Tourism and Special Events appointed an Arts Education Director to build stronger OST arts programs. In focusing on the summer months (which were coming up at the time) and on increasing the provision of arts programs, the new director relied on the previous mapping to target neighborhoods. He convened local arts education experts, including the arts coordinator from BASB, to develop ideal program attributes that he could use as criteria for examining the backgrounds and lesson plans of possible providers.

In addition, the Barr Foundation supported the work of an arts coordinator in BASB whose task was to describe the networks of arts learning provision within distinct Boston neighborhoods and to develop networks in each neighborhood that would help the arts—and arts education—flourish. The arts coordinator set up a cooperative for arts supplies (Provider's Arts Resource Center); she also developed a training guide for OST program providers to help them understand not only the resources that were available, but also the benefits of including arts learning in their programs. With others at BASB, she developed an annual fair for principals at which they could find out about programs available for OST in their neighborhoods and schools.

Finally, in response to numerous school requests for funds to support individual programs, the foundations and private donors pooled funding into the Edvestors Fund. This works as follows: Schools present their proposals to Edvestors Fund members in one- or two-day conferences, after which the funders determine which school and/ or other programs to support. Arts program proposals compete equally with all other proposals for funding from the Edvestors Fund.

Achievements to Date and Future Prospects

Interviewees claimed that the number of OST slots for children had doubled over the preceding few years. (Note, however, that not all of these programs included arts learning.) Despite the efforts put forth to increase provision of OST programs, however, citywide coordination was still lacking. Interviewees expressed the need for a brokering organization that could better coordinate opportunities for all children in the city.

At the time of our study, both past and current efforts to coordinate organizations in Boston had benefited from strong leaders and start-up funds from foundations. Indeed, many programs in place at the time were capable of supporting accelerated coordination if groups were able to come together more effectively or an individual or organizational leader were to emerge. However, some people noted that the interest of key players was flagging. The Boston Foundation had committed its resources to helping low-performing schools, moving away from supporting both OST and arts learning programs. Similarly, MASS2020, a public charity essential to the progress that had been made, was shifting its focus from OST programming to extended-learning schools. And although the Barr Foundation remained committed to arts learning, this area was but one aspect of its giving. Despite the multiple efforts described above, it appeared that the city would benefit from further collaboration as individual providers and supporters continued their struggles to connect with each other and build a more coordinated system.

Chicago

During our interviews in Chicago (October and November 2006), we found little collaborative effort other than that of a group of foundations supporting the school district's newly hired director for the arts (whose title changed to Director, Office of Arts Education, during our study). The city's many other networks of providers and influencers were involved in their own efforts, but there was little coordination across them.

Context and Motivation for Change

In 1979, Chicago Public Schools was hit by a fiscal crisis so severe that many arts specialist (and other) positions were cut from the budget (Rabkin and Redmond, 2004). This crisis also precipitated a reduction in the school day to just under six hours. In 1988, after a series of teacher strikes, the Illinois General Assembly passed the Chicago School Reform Act, giving the schools significant site-based authority. That same year, the Illinois Alliance for Arts Education produced standards for arts education. In 1992, Chicago Public Schools began to provide for 0.5 full-time equivalent arts teachers for every 700 to 750 students.

In the years after the decline of the arts programs, Chicago's arts education provider groups grew through sustained funding from local foundations such as the Jamee and Marshall Field Foundation and The Chicago Community Trust. Urban Gateways and CAPE created and sustained partnerships among schools, teachers, artists, and cultural organizations offering artist residencies, professional development, etc. The Center for Community Arts Partnerships, run out of Columbia College, also provided arts education experiences during and after school through local artists. These organizations grew over the years but reached fewer than half of the city's schools.

Chicago's OST scene has also grown, again with significant support from foundations; but the focus in this case has not been solely on the arts. At the time of our study, community-based organizations, such as After School Matters, the Chicago Parks District, and the 100 community schools (those structured and funded to provide additional services before, during, and after school), were offering an array of children's programs, only some of which were arts focused.

Even with these flourishing organizations and partnerships, there was dissatisfaction among the city's providers and influencers over uneven access to arts learning opportunities across the schools. In 2002, The Chicago Community Trust conducted a survey of arts education provision across schools and found that schools offered primarily visual arts and music and that provision was fragmented, unassessed, and random (Donaldson and Pearsall, 2002). Although most people surveyed knew standards existed, most teachers reported that they did not teach to the standards and that training was uneven. The survey also identified 144 different arts organizations that were providing artists or programs to schools with support from 200 foundations in the city, all without any coordination. Fortified with these facts, The Chicago Community Trust began a campaign to improve access across schools.

Coordination Goals and Efforts

The Chicago Community Trust leaders aspired to something more systematic and less idiosyncratic and questioned the wisdom of individual schools working with outside providers to offer arts integration experiences. In 2002, the trust launched a new initiative to develop a sequential arts demonstration program that would be provided in schools based on geographic clusters spread across the city specifically to capture a range of schools and students. In what represented a coordinated effort to fund systemic change, 13 local foundations aligned with the trust in supporting this initiative.

In the initiative's first year of implementation, the foundations selected four clusters and one individual school based on applications from interested schools that were geographically dispersed and served diverse populations. Only elementary schools were eligible. Schools received planning and then implementation grants, some of which required matched funding. A 40-member community task force oversaw this initiative.

The initiative was embedded in the system itself, as opposed to the more frequent practice of hiring local arts organizations to work with schools one at a time, and all money went directly to schools rather than to outside vendors. This approach brought its own obstacles, such as difficulties related to getting the funding to the schools, finding key people who could support the initiative from within the system, and dealing with turnover among these key supporters. The trust took stock of this program in 2004 and concluded that although progress had been made, the problem of random, unassessed programs spread across only a few schools was not being fixed. Indeed, the program was adding one more element to an already complicated mix.

Leaders of the trust began to view efforts in New York City and the Los Angeles Unified School District as ways to achieve greater change. The trust persuaded the Chicago school superintendent to hire a director for the arts, a key element of these two other efforts. This director was to sit in the superintendent's cabinet and lead an effort to provide all students in Chicago Public Schools with access to in-school, sequential, standards-based arts education in all four disciplines. The school district crafted an agreement with The Chicago Community Trust (and 17 other foundations and individuals, continuing the leveraged funding model) to share the cost of the search and the new director's salary for the first three years.

At the time of our visit (fall 2006), the new director had only recently been selected and was embarking on a state grant-funded strategic planning process for arts education. His title became Director, Office of Arts Education, when this new office was created around the same time. At the end of our study period, he held a staff position with minimal authority over school principals. The Office of Arts Education's budget was $1.3 million, 50 percent of which was dedicated for office staff salaries. The director did not control the larger share of funding that might be used for the arts (or other purposes)—that share was directly under the management of school principals.

Enthusiasm for this change was based in part on the idea that at least arts education would be represented in major policy discussions within school district headquarters. Although this position ended up not being at the cabinet level, it nonetheless represents progress in establishing an advocate for the arts at the level of the central school district office. The plan was that the funding collaborative led by The Chicago Community Trust would not only help fund this position, but would become an ongoing gift circle for bringing in vendors such as CAPE and the Chicago Arts Institute. Foundation leaders hoped that these organizations would maintain their involvement in the school district but within an organized structure. Foundation supporters hoped that the new director would work to align various efforts throughout the city, including the magnet and cluster schools, to bring about more-universal access.

Achievements to Date and Prospects for the Future

Despite a varied set of well-known providers, we found very little coordination in Chicago other than among the foundations, although many more-limited efforts were under way across the city to increase and improve arts learning experiences for children. Indeed, several individual providers reported that they had no desire to coordinate provision citywide and were content to provide deeper services to a few schools within the system. The most notable broad-scale change taking place was the 2006 appointment of the director that was funded by a consortium of foundations and givers.

We found two conditions in Chicago that we thought might hamper the new director's efforts to coordinate providers and ultimately provide arts learning experiences for all students. First, as interviewees noted, school principals were still in possession of important decisionmaking power in this system and would have to be convinced, along with lead teachers and local school councils, of the arts' value one by one. Second, as was revealed when interviewees were closely questioned, there were competing philosophies and approaches among the organizational actors in Chicago. Some community-based providers had developed integrated practices to fit arts learning into the narrow time and space afforded by the school day. Over time, many of these providers had come to see this as a preferred way to provide arts instruction (Burnaford, Aprill, and Weiss, 2001) and had worked to improve this form of provision. Moreover, having suffered the setbacks of the previous three decades, they did not trust Chicago Public Schools leaders to maintain arts programming. Thus, they argued for building networks of distributed leaders, advocates, and practitioners who could remain resilient in the face of barriers to provision and build stronger community support for arts learning over time. In their view, this approach supported greater resiliency and sustainability. Other respondents, however, envisioned a sequential standards-based approach with stand-alone courses throughout a student's schooling. Some providers and influencers within the city even viewed the integrated approaches as inferior and as supplemental to the arts as stand-alone courses. At the time of our visit, these two camps, while not at war, preferred to exist side by side. It was too early to predict whether the new director would be able to mesh these two approaches into a more coherent provision of arts education.

Dallas

In our visit to Dallas (October 2006), we focused on a community-based organization called Big Thought and its programmatic evolution, which culminated in the Dallas Arts Learning Initiative (DALI). In a ten-year period, all provider and influencer groups had become involved in Big Thought's citywide effort to improve arts education, and the initiative had attracted both local and national foundation funding.

Context and Motivation for Change

According to our interviewees, the provision of arts education had been dramatically reduced throughout the state of Texas by the late 1980s. Schools were facing incentives to improve pass rates on standardized achievement tests so that students would be allowed to participate in extracurricular activities.

In 1987, with seed funding from local foundations, three arts education advocates opened a Young Audiences chapter in Dallas that offered performances at schools, workshops for students, and a large artist in-school residency program. At that time, no other arts organizations trained artists to work in schools.

In 1995, the City of Dallas Office of Cultural Affairs initiated conversations with Young Audiences of North Texas and other local community-based providers on the subject of working collaboratively to systemically improve access to arts education for all children in the city. Together, these groups conducted an audit to determine what arts experiences were being offered at which schools. The audit produced preliminary evidence that approximately one-third of Dallas Independent School District schools (those in high-income areas) were high resourced, one-third offered art or music about once a month, and one-third (those in the highest-poverty areas) provided nothing. Leaders of these different organizations publicized the results, emphasizing the neighborhood-based inequity of provision. Thus began a more formal commitment, based on equity concerns, to improve arts education.

In 1998, the state signaled renewed support for the arts by adopting the Texas Essential Knowledge and Skills for the Fine Arts. Our interviewees reported that while high schools were adhering to the graduation requirement of one arts credit, many elementary and middle schools were not complying with state guidelines for instruction in the arts.

Coordination Goals and Efforts

In 1997, the Office of Cultural Affairs committed $50,000 to rectify the provision inequity based on neighborhood, and the Dallas Independent School District committed another $50,000. This funding launched ArtsPartners, a public-private partnership and an outgrowth of Young Audiences of North Texas, whose goal was to provide an integrated arts learning experience to all elementary students in the school district and whose funding came from the district, the city, and private donors. ArtPartners started with 13 schools, one from each ward in the city. Each school received funding to purchase direct services for students in exchange for participating in the design of an improvement plan.

During a ten-year period, the leaders of Young Audiences accumulated arts programs, donors, and partners in addition to ArtsPartners. Young Audiences directed its programming at diverse populations, such as youth in the juvenile justice system, library goers, and pre-schoolers. ArtsPartners provided mostly in-school programming; it also served as a broker between arts organizations and the school district, managing the contracting, invoicing, and payment processes. In the early 2000s, the directors of Young Audiences recognized that the various programs and services they were overseeing would benefit from a larger, more expansive organizational name and structure.

Big Thought,[3] incorporated to serve this purpose in 2004, provided ArtsPartners and its other tenant programs with many services, including program design, private-sector fundraising, governance, and fiscal management.

Big Thought has received funding from local business donors (e.g., American Airlines, Bank of America, IBM), national foundations (e.g., The Ford Foundation), arts agencies (the NEA, Texas Commission on the Arts, etc.), and local foundations. In addition, the school district and the City of Dallas Office of Cultural Affairs have remained faithful funders.

To create this pool of funds and the private-public partnership, leaders had to convince all partner organizations—including the community-based providers, OST and cultural organizations, and city departments—that they would be better off using a coordinated organizational and funding mechanism than applying individually for separate funding.

The leadership of Big Thought has been credited with an inclusive and engaging style. As one member put it when discussing how Big Thought's leaders approached the task of building stronger partners across the community: "In that environment (of high-stakes testing on reading and math), we had to have multiple stakeholders at multiple levels, because people changed jobs every six months. This was a very deliberate strategy of having multiple heads, multiple support, and some inside and some outside—and from every level, starting from teachers up."

Big Thought successfully applied to The Ford Foundation for funding to develop greater public support for arts education that favored an integrated approach. It used the award to engage parents and the general community in its development of advocates for arts education. A staff member of Big Thought said, "Our role became advocacy and educating the community on the value of the arts, not the value of Big Thought."

In 2006, The Wallace Foundation approached Big Thought with an investment opportunity: It challenged Big Thought to develop a plan for expanding its services. The ensuing planning process, which stretched across multiple organizations, culminated in Big Thought's launching of DALI in February 2007.[4] While coordinated approaches and budding partnerships had begun under ArtsPartners, the creation of DALI began a new level of coordinated effort within the community of Dallas arts education providers to improve access to arts learning experiences. DALI has been a partnership among city, district, and local community-based providers and cultural organizations. At the time of our study, the DALI leadership committee included the Big Thought executive director and board president; the city manager, mayor, and deputy mayor; the district superintendent and a board member; and representatives of local chambers of commerce.

---

[3]   Big Thought's Web site is (as of January 1, 2008) http://www.bigthought.org.

[4]   The DALI Web site (as of December 26, 2007) is http://www.dallasartslearning.org.

With support from Wallace, Big Thought convened players throughout the city in a series of visioning and planning exercises. Working in committees over several months, they decided on three strands for DALI: standards-based instruction in all public elementary schools; arts and cultural integration to support both classroom teachers and arts specialists at the elementary level; OST provision for all youth and their family members. The third of these strands heavily involved the city departments of parks and recreation and libraries, as well as community centers, in a neighborhood-level arts education initiative.

Wallace then provided a three-year, $8 million grant to Big Thought to manage DALI. Big Thought was matching this amount through local fundraising efforts; for example, Bank of America provided $1 million toward the initiative. The public sector—the school district, the City of Dallas Office of Cultural Affairs, and the U.S. Department of Education—provided approximately $17 million. In total, DALI represented a $39.8 million program.

DALI has continued the arts integration work of over 50 community-based providers through ArtsPartners, and at the time of our study, Big Thought was planning to improve the quality of these integration experiences. Additionally, DALI was supporting the school district's efforts to expand sequential in-school courses and was working with a new Executive Director of Fine Arts to advocate for hiring arts specialists and developing a strong sequential arts curriculum. DALI's ambitions centered on launching significant new OST opportunities that would be embedded in distinct communities across the city. Big Thought was considering the use of programs that constitute "gateway" arts experiences, the idea being to offer these programs and then expand into more-traditional arts experiences. It was thought that gateway experiences might include programs on sewing, pet care, personal grooming, gardening, fashion, or cosmetology. Such programs would be offered in as many as 20 distinct neighborhoods, each with its own cultural personality, and each neighborhood would have a "hub" that provides both information and programming. Local staff would canvas neighborhoods to determine needs and coordinate program offerings.

Achievements to Date and Prospects for the Future

Through the efforts of Young Audiences, ArtsPartners, and now Big Thought, access to arts learning experiences in Dallas has steadily increased. At the time of our study, Big Thought was managing Young Audiences, ArtsPartners, and other long-standing tenant programs, as well as DALI, partnering with more than 70 community agencies—such as the school district, library systems, child care centers, recreation centers, and juvenile detention facilities—to improve access to quality arts learning programs for children across the city.

After ten years of coordinated efforts, all elementary school students in Dallas were being exposed to arts learning experiences, and the district was planning to hire 140 new arts specialists to serve all elementary grade levels. There were significant levels of collaboration across the entire ecology of the arts education sector, with conversations on quality evolving collaboratively. Furthermore, most of the planned expansions to increase access had been funded. Therefore, it was likely that DALI would continue to be supported over time.

Los Angeles County

In visiting Los Angeles County (fall 2006 and winter 2006–07), we focused on the countywide effort known as Arts for All: Los Angeles County Regional Blueprint for Arts Education (Los Angeles County Arts Commission, undated-a). Similar to the Alameda County effort, the one in Los Angeles County was being led by a county-level organization and had involved an array of providers and influencers over a five-year period.

Context and Motivation for Change

In reaction to the 1978 passage of Proposition 13, many Los Angeles County school districts cut their budgets by removing music, drama, dance, and visual arts from the schools. The delivery of arts education programs grew sporadic and inequitable.

In 1993, a coalition of arts and arts education advocates across Los Angeles County began meeting regularly to strategize on advocacy for public support of the arts. Members of the coalition suspected that access to arts education in the county's school districts was uneven. In 2000, the Los Angeles County Arts Commission, whose leaders and staff were part of the coalition, commissioned and partially funded a survey of arts education throughout the county.[5] Data were collected through in-person interviews with officials from 80 of the then 82 school districts. The results, released in May 2001, provided baseline data on arts education. They showed wide variation in the degree to which the arts were included in curricula across schools in the county. Results were shared with stakeholders in community forums in what became a year-long, community-based strategic planning process focused on arts education, a first step in efforts to better coordinate improvement within the county. During our case-study visit, interviewees argued that this lengthy convening step was key and that it elicited leaders from the stakeholders that would have been difficult to identify otherwise. Efforts then focused on improving access across the districts and schools.

Also in 2001, California's State Board of Education adopted content standards for visual and performing arts, thereby signaling renewed support for arts education. Five years later, the state announced a new categorical funding stream of just over $100 million to support the implementation of sequential, standards-aligned instruction in

---

[5]   The results are documented in *Arts in Focus: Los Angeles Countywide Arts Education Survey* (Museums Without Walls, Los Angeles, 2001).

the arts in grades K–12 (California Department of Education, 2007). In addition, the state provided a one-time apportionment of $500 million for equipment, supplies, and professional development to support arts, music, and physical fitness education. Funding was allocated to central school district offices. Many of our interviewees expressed hope that the arts would be restored in California's schools. Many also believed that restoration of the arts would be challenging given the lack of arts education in most schools over the previous 30 years (Woodworth, Gallagher, and Guha, 2007).

Coordination Goals and Efforts

These community-based strategic planning efforts culminated in a design for improving access to arts education across the county. In July 2002, the Los Angeles County Board of Supervisors adopted Arts for All: Los Angeles County Regional Blueprint for Arts Education, a ten-year strategic plan to restore sequential, standards-based arts education—in dance, music, theater, and visual arts—to the 1.7 million students in Los Angeles County's 80 school districts (Los Angeles County Arts Commission, 2002). A representative from Arts for All stressed that when the initiative was launched, there was general recognition in the arts education community that money spent on community-based providers had not led to systemic access to arts education in schools. Therefore, the focus of the new efforts was to be on assisting school districts in developing budgets, personnel, and policies to support arts education within their districts.

At the time of our study, an Arts for All executive committee was leading this effort. Representatives of the Los Angeles County Arts Commission and the Los Angeles County Office of Education served on this committee, along with county-level elected officials, local business executives, the director of the California Alliance for Arts Education, and an executive of a local arts education provider. The Los Angeles County Arts Commission, in conjunction with the Los Angeles County Office of Education, provided dedicated staff time in support of the initiative. At the time of our site visit, this committee was "virtual" (i.e., it had no office space or full-time leadership).

Arts for All emphasized the building of infrastructure in the county's school districts to support comprehensive, standards-based, sequential arts education offered within the school day. Districts would decide whether to institute stand-alone arts courses or to provide sequential instruction via integration of the arts into other disciplines.

Arts for All's strategic plan had four goals:

1. Each of the 80 school districts in Los Angeles County (and the Los Angeles County Office of Education classrooms) would enact a policy, adopt a plan with timeline, hire a district-level arts coordinator, approve a 5 percent district budget allocation to implement sequential K–12 arts education, and hire a sufficient number of arts specialists to achieve at least a 400:1 ratio of students to credentialed arts teachers.

2. Implementers and policymakers would have sufficient tools, information, and professional development to achieve sequential K–12 arts education.
3. Each of the 80 school districts would mobilize an active coalition of advocates to establish, sustain, and support sequential K–12 arts education.
4. Funding policies of public and private donors would support and align with the vision and mission of this plan.

Arts for All was supported by a pooled fund that was established in 2004 with a $500,000 gift and fostered by the leadership of one of the executive committee members. This fund supported technical assistance training and key components of districts' plans. Close to $1.5 million had been committed at the time of our study, matched by $1.5 million from participating school districts. Donors included local foundations, local businesses, and national corporations. Together the donors served as a governing board, meeting quarterly to vote on how to allocate the pooled funds.

Starting in 2003–04, the Arts for All executive committee invited selected school districts to receive multi-year technical assistance. These districts and subsequent cohorts received coaching to support planning and some implementation of their plans. In response to new state funding in California, Arts for All recast its original technical assistance model in the winter of 2006–07. All school districts not already participating in Arts for All were offered a choice of three technical assistance models whose (subsidized) costs were based on level of service selected and size of school district. All district-level arts coordinators became eligible for training through Arts for All. In addition to supporting school district planning and implementation, Arts for All also supported artist in-school residencies.

Achievements to Date and Prospects for the Future
The establishment of Arts for All represented achievements in data collection, fundraising, and infrastructure building by dedicated leaders. The most important achievement was that school districts in Los Angeles County began aligning themselves with Arts for All and developing and implementing plans to improve arts education. After six years of coordinated efforts to improve access to arts education, 19 school districts were being served under the original, or old, Arts for All model, and nine had signed up for one of the three new models. This means that one-third of the school districts in Los Angeles County were participating in Arts for All—i.e., were developing or implementing a plan to provide arts learning experiences to all students in their districts.

Arts for All leaders were planning to continue to expand, their efforts bolstered by recent new state funds. However, we identified at least two potential obstacles to continued expansion.

First, the capacity to meet the increasing demand for Arts for All services may be insufficient. Interviewees stressed that the school districts being worked with were needing more support than Arts for All leaders had anticipated and that the districts' capacity for providing arts education was turning out to be lower than had been believed. At the same time, new school districts were joining Arts for All each year. Providing sufficient support to both the existing and the new school districts will thus be an ongoing challenge. Second, Arts for All was attracting districts that were willing, interested, and ready to join the initiative. Eventually, however, Arts for All leaders will have to develop mechanisms to incentivize districts that previously were not ready to focus on arts education. It is too soon to tell whether the new state funding alone will provide an adequate incentive for these districts.

New York

For our New York City interviews (March 2007), we focused on the public school system's effort to coordinate improved access to arts education—called the Step-Up initiative and supported by a grant from The Wallace Foundation—in the city's schools. As in Chicago, this effort was led from within the school district and did not evolve to include the city's numerous providers and influencers in a fully collaborative network.

Context and Motivation for Change

After a decade of constant budget cuts, the New York City schools laid off 15,000 teachers in 1975–76. Schools were no longer encouraged to hire arts specialists, and positions in the central school district office dedicated to arts education were reduced. Community-based providers, such as ArtsConnection and Studio in a School, began to develop what was thought to be transitional provision of arts learning during this time of crisis, their support coming primarily from local funders, including foundations. But the decline in arts instruction turned out to be more enduring: "By 1991, the last year for which systematic arts data was collected by the Board of Education, two-thirds of the schools had no licensed art or music teachers" (CAE, 2007, p. 10).

New community-based providers sprang up to fill the void, and cultural organizations improved and increased their educational programming. As a result, New York City became home to some of the best-known programs in the nation. Together these groups reportedly provided $37 million in services to New York City's public schools, including more than $25 million for education programs (New York City Arts in Education Roundtable, 2006). New York City also became home to arts education advocacy organizations such as ArtsVision and CAE, whose mission was to restore, stimulate, and sustain the systemic return of arts education to the city's public schools.

In 1997, when the city budget finally had some slack, the mayor's office recognized the widespread support for restoring arts education and funded the creation of Project Arts, a categorical fund of $25 million to support arts in the schools. Within two years, this funding was increased to $75 million. Over time, changes in leadership affected the level and manner of funding. After New York City's mayor gained control of the public schools in 2002, he changed the administrative structure significantly. In 2003, the city decreased funding to $67.5 million per year for Project Arts and distributed the funds evenly to schools at a rate of $63.44 per student to eliminate inequities across schools.

Also in 2003, the schools were charged with refocusing the arts, and three major efforts were undertaken. First, an Office of Arts and Special Projects was established and, over the course of several months, staffed with a Senior Instructional Manager for Arts Education and four directors, one each for dance, music, theater, and visual arts. This office assumed responsibility for creating guidelines for the use of Project Arts funds. Second, this team worked with experts from universities, community-based providers, and cultural organizations throughout the city to develop "the Blueprints"—arts education guidelines matched to the New York state standards (New York City Department of Education, 2004). Third, the staff began to focus on hiring arts specialists and offering professional development in the Blueprints to all schools. Those schools with high interest in the arts worked with their regional arts supervisors to provide additional professional development and other opportunities to improve.

All of our interviewees agreed that arts education provision within New York City's public schools was still highly erratic, varying significantly from school to school and across grades. This situation has been exacerbated by a lack of arts teachers: "Although about 40,000 teachers have been added to the New York City school system since 1975—bringing the current total to about 84,000—no more than 2,000 of them are arts specialists. . . . [I]t would cost $150 million to $200 million to hire arts specialists for every school" (Pogrebin, 2006).

Coordination Goals and Efforts

In 2005, The Wallace Foundation approached the New York City Department of Education with a request for a proposal for a planning grant to improve arts learning. The grant was to be used to help establish a more coordinated system of arts learning using in-school time and OST, and the education department was expected to coordinate improvement efforts with other organizations across the city. The department responded with a proposal led by the Office of Arts and Special Projects with a team from the Fund for Public Schools, Department of Cultural Affairs, and CAE. The proposal called for a ten-month planning period to gather information on the current state of arts education and develop a plan; it also promised to involve multiple partners and to bridge in-school and OST arts learning providers to bring community resources into a coordinated effort. The goal was to have each school, over a phased three-year period, enter into a consultancy process, called Step-Up, with the education department in order to develop plans for both infusing the arts into the school and meeting standards. At the end of this process, all schools would be providing quality arts education experiences or would have plans to do so. The New York City Department of Education was given the grant and began its planning for the Step-Up process.

As part of the planning process, schools were surveyed to gather information on courses and enrollment. The survey showed uneven participation in arts learning throughout the system. For example, 86 percent of middle schools taught two arts forms, but only 50 percent of their students enrolled in the courses. Those schools offering English as a Second Language programs or other additional required classes reported that there was no time in the day for the arts. Elementary schools were supposed to be offering four arts forms, but only 25 percent of them reported doing so. The survey also established that approximately 150 schools had no full-time arts specialists.

According to observers outside the education department, after the initiative got off to a promising start with several meetings and the involvement of many actors, the Office of Arts and Special Projects' implementation of the planning grant appeared to concentrate on continued hiring of arts specialists for the public schools and increased professional development for teachers in the Blueprint. Non-department interviewees noted that efforts to involve outside providers appeared to be relegated to a lower priority, along with OST provision. It appeared that little effort was going into building partnerships with the very vibrant arts community and the extensive arts education community outside the schools.

The Step-Up initiative was further stalled, in April 2007, when the Chancellor of the New York City Department of Education changed policy and announced a new plan: The ten regional superintendent offices, along with the regional arts supervisors, would be eliminated by September 2007, and school principals would be given significant autonomy in selecting school support organizations and determining curriculum. Furthermore, Project Arts funding would be rolled into the larger budgets for schools in the 2007–08 school year, thus removing categorical funding for arts education. Many in the arts education community told us they believed that principals, facing strong accountability for reading and mathematics and given no categorical arts funding or regional district support, would further reduce the provision of arts education in their schools. Many of our respondents predicted that absent a strong collaboration with partners outside the schools, the Step-Up initiative would collapse. As of October 2007, no definitive decisions about the initiative had been made.

Achievements to Date and Prospects for the Future

The history of this effort offers a counterexample to some of the other histories. The Office of Arts and Special Projects was planning to continue its school surveys, but there was no way to know whether principals, given their new autonomy, would continue to support the arts as they had under categorical funding. Some feared that many of the small community-based providers would not survive an arts education downscaling. The Office of Arts and Special Projects, however, was hopeful not only that the level of resources dedicated to arts education would remain at least stable, but also that schools would be held accountable for providing quality arts learning experiences. It was not yet clear at the time of our visit how this accountability would occur.

Summary

This chapter has detailed the context for and evolution of coordinated efforts to improve access to arts learning experiences at six sites. Arts education experts and collected information on arts education efforts led us to expect that these six sites would offer "something interesting" in collaborative approaches to building better arts education systems. As it turned out, however, some of them did not involve much collaboration and/or were not focused predominantly on arts education. To us, this is a strong indication that the knowledge base on community efforts to improve arts education is simply not there. Much more could be done to share knowledge of practices across communities to the mutual benefit of cities around the nation that are attempting to build better arts education systems.

Nevertheless, we did find that the six sites had much in common in types of providers and influencers, histories of downturns caused by budget issues, changes brought about by test-based accountability, and the idiosyncratic and poor provision of arts education that resulted. They all also had a very rich set of assets that could be drawn on to build a collaborative effort. One major separating issue in the cases appears to be whether a leader(s) with a unifying vision and organizational and collaborative adeptness emerges from the particular circumstances to better deploy existing assets across organizations and enable the growth of new, necessary assets.

Closer inspection showed that the details of the sites' environments and the specific views of important parties influenced the paths that sites took toward collaborative efforts. We found that these collaborative efforts were quite "local," with the strengths and weaknesses of specific actors and organizations greatly influencing the choices and progress made. The six sites varied in their focus on in-school versus OST provision of arts education, as well as in whether provision would take the form of stand-alone courses or arts integration. They also varied in governance structures, policies, and funding, which clearly made a difference in their choices and how the effort proceeded.

We found that three of the sites, Alameda and Los Angeles counties and Dallas, had functioning collaborations only after at least five years of effort and only under the auspices of community-based or county-based organizations. Within this small sample of six, efforts that were lodged in the central office of a large school district had difficulty reaching out to external partners to build collaborations and suffered when funding was short or cut. These patterns and the others we found are discussed in the next two chapters, which further explore lessons we can learn from the case studies about how to begin collaboration and how to sustain it.

CHAPTER FOUR

Strategies for Improving Access and Quality

This chapter describes the most prevalent strategies used by our six case studies to improve both access to and quality of children's arts learning experiences. Some strategies were used to improve either access or quality; others, such as strategic planning and capacity building, were used to improve both. We begin by describing these strategies in the order in which they were implemented in the sites, but it should be noted that many of them were pursued simultaneously or iteratively. We then discuss why the sites employed these strategies and how they implemented them. We also point out tensions and limitations inherent in these strategies.

Strategies to Improve Access

At all of the sites, interviewees pointed out that high-quality arts education programs have existed in their schools and communities for many years. We selected our case studies partly because of their reputations for concerted, coordinated efforts to improve access to these quality experiences. The coordination efforts in the six sites were at different stages at the time of our study: They were just beginning in Chicago and Boston, they were changing course in New York City, and they were at a point where they could provide evidence of having improved access to arts learning experiences in Alameda and Los Angeles counties and Dallas.

Across the sites, we observed different strategies in use for improving access. The eight most prevalent were as follows:

1. conducting audits of arts education
2. setting a goal of access for all
3. strategic planning
4. constructing a case
5. attracting and leveraging resources
6. hiring an arts education coordinator highly placed within the school district administration

7. building individual and organizational capacity

8. advocating.

Conducting Audits of Arts Education

The sites used audits to gather information on how many students were served by arts learning programs by school, neighborhood, or region. Respondents indicated that this information was useful for several purposes, including highlighting inequities in provision in order to galvanize funders and policymakers, and establishing plans to fill gaps in provision. Audits often served as the first step in igniting coordinated efforts to improve access.

All sites except Alameda County conducted audits to determine how many children were served throughout their region. All of these audits except Boston's focused on in-school provision. In Boston, foundations supported the mapping of OST opportunities against incidences of violence to determine opportunities for expanded provision.

Leaders of the various coordination efforts used different approaches for the school-level audits in Chicago, Dallas, Los Angeles County, and New York City. The Chicago Community Trust conducted a survey in 2002. In Dallas, Young Audience leaders worked with the city's Office of Cultural Affairs to analyze data from the city school district in 1997. In Los Angeles County, the County Arts Commission commissioned interviews with each of 82 district superintendents in 2000. In New York City, the District Office of Arts and Special Projects audited arts specialists and courses in 2006.[1]

Audits in these four sites all revealed similar patterns: Access to arts education in these regions was inequitable. In Dallas, arts education provision was more prevalent in wealthier areas of the city. In Chicago, Los Angeles County, and New York City, arts education provision depended on the values, proclivities, and skills of district superintendents and school principals. All four sites had high-quality arts education programs, but students' access to these programs depended on the school they attended and was, at best, idiosyncratic.

Leaders in these four sites reported using audit results to galvanize support for more-equitable provision of arts education and to launch coordinated efforts to overcome inequities. The Illinois Arts Alliance conducted a similar audit throughout the state of Illinois and heavily publicized the results, leading, in the opinion of its officials, to state funding of planning grants for districts to improve student access to arts learning. Young Audiences, in Dallas, used its audit results to rouse the district into providing seed funding for ArtsPartners. Survey results for Los Angeles County were widely publicized and used to persuade funders to support Arts for All.

---

[1] Funding received from The Wallace Foundation allowed this office to collect information on arts education in schools that had never before been collected.

Although all of these sites reported that their audits were useful, we noted that the audit approaches were not equivalent to each other—for example, some data used were longitudinal, some were from a single point in time, some were quantitative, and some were qualitative surveys/self-reports.

Setting a Goal of Access for All

Many leaders of the coordinated efforts in our six sites perceived arts education as a social justice issue, arguing that uneven access is unfair. In all sites, individual organizations (e.g., Chicago Public Schools) or coordinating bodies (e.g., Alliance for Arts Learning Leadership) had established a goal to provide quality arts learning experiences to either all children in school (Alameda and Los Angeles counties) or children in general (Dallas). Most sites used the results of the audits to secure buy-in on this goal from other providers and influencers, including funders.

Leaders reported that establishing this goal was an important first step to improved access to arts learning. If the sites did not intentionally work toward access for all children, they reasoned, then access for all would be highly improbable given the idiosyncratic nature of current in-school and OST arts learning provision. They thought that equal access to arts learning would be prevented from coming about naturally because of the current heavy emphasis on test scores in subjects other than the arts, the lack of time for arts learning during the school day, and uneven participation in OST programs.

Strategic Planning

Most of the sites were in the midst of ongoing strategic planning efforts. Alameda County's Alliance for Arts Learning Leadership had funding from The Ford Foundation to support ongoing strategic planning sessions aimed at setting strategies for increasing access. The new Director, Office of Arts Education, in the Chicago Public Schools was involved in strategic planning funded by a state arts education planning grant. Big Thought, in Dallas, had just concluded a planning effort, funded by Wallace, that produced a new plan for delivering expanded services to children and their families across the city. Arts for All, in Los Angeles County, had recently held retreats to strategically plan how to improve services to districts because of new state funding being received for arts education. And New York City's Department of Education had recently concluded a planning process, also funded by The Wallace Foundation.

Constructing a Case

For our study, constructing a case, or case-making, means building an argument for why a school, district, or other organization should provide or support arts education. This particular strategy draws on other strategies, such as establishing a goal of access for all, and supports other strategies, such as attracting resources and conducting advocacy. Case-making is important because decisionmakers, faced with scarce resources, must rely on it in deciding among competing priorities in school and OST settings. Furthermore, because decisionmakers are accountable to governing boards, parents, and others, the importance of case-making often extends further, to more-general stakeholders.

Most of our sites deliberately developed arguments for arts education to garner stakeholder support. Some sites advanced multiple reasons for providing children with arts learning experiences, including that arts education would engage students and thus motivate them to remain in and succeed in school, and would engender greater societal economic benefits as well as participation in and sustainability of the arts.

Some site leaders had hired professional case-making firms. Members of the Alliance for Arts Learning Leadership, in Alameda County, partnered with professional messaging firms to craft specific wording and phrases, for example. Leaders of this alliance then trained parents and others to use this vocabulary in pursuit of a common language to describe and convince others of the benefits of arts education.

Attracting and Leveraging Resources

At all of our sites, the resources available for arts education varied. Schools lacked time, qualified teachers, sufficient space and materials, and, perhaps most important of all, dedicated funding for arts education. According to district and foundation respondents, principals assigning priorities to subjects in schools often did so based on their own values and judgments. And if they chose to support the arts, they needed to be highly skilled at attracting and leveraging scarce resources to maintain arts education programs.

Community-based providers, also short on resources, reported that they often survived from grant to grant. Many realized that they needed dedicated fundraising operations to remain viable but often could not afford to hire experienced development staff or provide such staff with appropriate support.

In consequence, most organizations in our sites scrambled to attract resources. Respondents thought it important to seek resources early in an endeavor so that the organization could set realistic plans and have confidence in them. Within some sites, creative approaches to leveraging funds emerged. In Chicago, for example, 17 local foundations and individuals jointly funded half of the salary and benefits for the new Director, Office of Arts Education, for three years. The view of these foundations was that the district would not dedicate funding for a high-level arts education leader in the absence of this external support. In Los Angeles County, Arts for All created a pooled fund with contributions from ten to 15 organizations each year. Contributors make up a board that convenes quarterly to vote on how to spend the money; all contributors' votes are equal regardless of amount contributed. These funders, who reported high levels of satisfaction with this arrangement, believed that their donations leveraged systemic change rather than merely supporting individual local arts education programs that might never wean themselves from outside funding. As a leader of this initiative reported:

> No one has enough money to put arts education back in schools, so all of us have to be very strategic. The pooled fund helps us see how to aggregate resources but also provides an opportunity for all funders. We have to decide together about the highest priorities. We all make a contribution to the pooled fund but also are contributing to arts education in a different, more coordinated way.

Big Thought, in Dallas, had an experienced fundraising staff and had succeeded in raising both local and national dollars for arts education. Its early, local success brought national foundation interest; it then leveraged its national funding to obtain additional local funding. Receiving a large grant from The Wallace Foundation facilitated Big Thought's ability to attract other funds and gain broad support from the business community, the school district, and the city administration.

The Alliance for Arts Learning Leadership, in Alameda County, had also been successful in attracting both local and national foundation dollars. Community-based providers active in this alliance were thrilled with their recent grant wins, which they attributed to having proposed them in partnership with local schools and other providers. These partnerships came about because of the schools' and the providers' association with the alliance.

In Los Angeles County, an external organization was providing seed funding to districts as an incentive to join the network and develop and implement arts education plans. Financial incentives can be powerful motivators for change, particularly for resource-strapped school districts. Although we did see evidence that schools accepted funding without fully committing to developing "high-quality" arts education programs, the coupling of financial incentives with matched funding had worked well in developing at least the initial buy-in.

Hiring an Arts Education Coordinator Highly Placed Within the School District Administration

Our sites either had an arts education coordinator position at the district level or were working to ensure there would be one. Positions had been established over the past ten years, the most recent being Chicago's new Director, Office of Arts Education, which was filled in 2006. Some districts in the two California counties were still moving toward this goal. The two county sites expected districts to hire or appoint an arts coordinator if they wanted to become a partner district. The rationale behind establishing an arts coordination position is that district-level arts education officials can advocate for the arts and secure a place for them in the district's core curriculum. A leader of Arts for All, in Los Angeles County, stated that

[the] arts will suffer if we simply hire an arts teacher out of the classroom on special assignment. The traditional model is to hire a teacher to do part-time coordination of the arts. I don't think you can have someone with no status in schools recharge arts education. We need to engage at a higher level. I feel a great sense of urgency, fragility with this. . . . We have to make sure that the arts become embedded alongside other district priorities. Low-level arts coordinators have no clout, no rank; they're locked out of key conversations and have low sophistication. Arts remain fragmented and isolated, at a lower level; . . . districts need a senior person. . . . We need that senior-level commitment. . . . It is very intimate, local, as to how to make that happen. It is about securing ownership, involvement, etc., of senior leadership, especially in secondary schools. . . . We want someone at a higher level doing integrated thinking.

District coordinators can also establish support infrastructure, such as dedicated budgets, curriculum frameworks, and professional development programs, that may lead to improved access for all students. In most of our sites, outside organizations—such as Arts for All, Alliance for Arts Learning Leadership, and The Chicago Community Trust–led Funding Coalition—persuaded or provided incentives to districts to fill district management positions dedicated to the arts.

Building Individual and Organizational Capacity

All of the sites had engaged in the important strategy of building existing teacher, administrator, and artist capacity to improve access to arts education. Given that many principals and teachers did not experience arts education when they were students, it is important to train arts teachers, regular classroom teachers, and teaching artists to help ensure they understand the value of arts education and feel prepared to teach it. According to one leader of Arts for All:

Schools are afraid to teach the arts. Teachers are arts phobic. They're afraid we want them to be the full-time music teacher. We can teach them music without them being an accomplished pianist. Dance teachers say they can't dance; [but] if they get specific examples and coaching, they can do it. The teachers don't have to dance anyway—the kids do. We can train a teacher to teach dance.

Several respondents told us that the high rates of turnover for administrators and teachers make this work ongoing.

Within each of the sites, different organizations offered professional development and technical assistance to schools to assist teachers in arts education provision and administrators in planning for, supporting, and providing leadership for arts education. Among those offering professional development and coaching were state and county agencies, local education agencies, and local community-based providers (such as CAPE and ArtsConnection). Many of these local community-based providers had professional development programs that engaged partner schools in improving not only their arts education programs, but pedagogy in general, as well as school culture. Although many professional development experiences were being offered through one-on-one partnerships, schools were given opportunities to come together in institute settings or district meetings to share best practices and lessons learned.

There were also opportunities for artists and arts organizations to participate in professional development. In Los Angeles County, Arts for All hosted annual sessions for local artists, training them to develop lesson plans that aligned with California's state standards and were developmentally appropriate for various age groups. These artists also learned to provide technical assistance to teachers in classrooms. In Alameda County, Alliance for Arts Learning Leadership also provided training opportunities for artists. In Dallas, community-based providers were given the opportunity to evaluate lesson plans developed by peer arts organizations in conjunction with schools as part of a regular, ongoing, lesson-plan scoring system used to qualify programs for ArtsPartner funding. This process facilitates learning about other providers' curricula.

Finally, efforts were being made in Alameda County to increase the number of new teachers entering the field with arts education training. The Alliance for Arts Learning Leadership was building a relationship with a consortium of six universities in the region (the Arts Education Initiative, funded by The Ford Foundation) to improve pre-service teacher preparation and create a pipeline of new teachers prepared to teach in and through the arts.

Advocating

Many of our interviewees stressed that arts education needs constant advocacy. Key decisionmakers (superintendents, principals, OST coordinators, and funders) often need to be convinced of the value of the arts. Even in states mandating specified time for arts education, schools admitted to being out of compliance because of competing priorities. Mandates that are unfunded and lack accountability mechanisms are often rendered meaningless by other, strict accountability mechanisms. Hence, interviewees thought there was an ongoing need for advocacy at the local level.

Advocacy may affect access to arts education both directly and indirectly: directly, by generating changes to policies and funding; and indirectly, by spurring students, parents, teachers, principals, and others to request it of their community leaders. For example, representatives from the Alliance for Arts Learning Leadership argue that quality exhibitions and performances of arts learning fuel advocacy initiatives. The alliance hosts a countywide showcase of student learning in and through the arts that has two aims: to communicate the value of arts learning for equitable education outcomes and to generate new parent and educator advocates for access to arts learning for every child in every school every day.

Note that although the strategy of advocacy was implemented in our sites as one of the first steps in establishing coordinated efforts, it is an ongoing strategy, necessary throughout the life of efforts to improve access to arts education.

Interviewees in four of the sites discussed their strategies for advocating for arts education. The leaders of coordinated efforts in two of the sites told us that they rely on formal advocacy organizations for most of this work. Arts for All had recently contracted with an advocacy organization called Arts Los Angeles. The foundation community in Chicago was working very closely with the Illinois Arts Alliance to advocate for the arts and arts education in the state legislature. In two other sites, the leaders of the regional coordination efforts were also the primary advocates. Members of both the Alliance for Arts Learning Leadership and Big Thought were conducting sophisticated advocacy campaigns targeting local and state policymakers.

The primary focus of these advocacy campaigns differed by site. Arts for All had engaged Arts Los Angeles to track local school district elections. This organization was to determine who was running for the school board in each of the 80 local districts and identify those candidates willing to promote arts education once elected.

In both Chicago and Alameda County, advocacy efforts mainly focused on increasing state funding for arts education. The Illinois Arts Alliance and the Alliance for Arts Learning Leadership claimed partial credit for their respective states' recent provision of additional funding for arts education. A representative from the Illinois Arts Alliance described advocating for arts education funding as easier than advocating for other arts funding; she attributed the relative ease to the fact that many state representatives, having engaged in arts learning in their youth, are concerned about its decline in the schools.

The Alameda County alliance considered advocacy to be a daily core activity. Members trained students, parents, teachers, principals, and district administrators in messaging for the arts and advocacy in general. In line with their own definition of quality arts learning, they were attempting to improve individuals' advocacy skills, motivation to advocate, and, in particular, alertness to potential advocacy "moments."

In Dallas, Big Thought spent its time advocating not only with leaders of local and state organizations, but also with their "deputies"—those next in line for positions of power. Big Thought leaders argued that going one or two steps down in each organization is useful for ensuring that tomorrow's leaders are today's arts education supporters. They had also begun working with parents and communities to better understand their needs and to encourage them to advocate on behalf of arts education.

Note that although we have described these advocacy efforts as discrete events centered within regions, cross-over advocacy does occur. In partnership with the California Alliance for Arts Education, Alameda County's Alliance for Arts Learning Leadership has collaborated with Los Angeles County's Arts for All and other such county organizations throughout the state to advocate for arts education across the state.

Progress on Access

In Dallas, after ten years of coordinated efforts, all elementary-level students had the opportunity for arts learning experiences, and there were plans to hire 140 new arts specialists for the elementary level. In Alameda County, after eight years of coordinated work, over 70 percent of the county's school districts were involved in the Alliance for Arts Learning Leadership, either developing or implementing a plan to serve all students in their district. In Los Angeles County, after five years of coordination, 19 school districts were being served under the old model, and nine had signed up for one of the three new models.[2] One-third of the districts in Los Angeles County were thus participating in Arts for All, which means they were either developing or implementing a plan to provide arts learning experiences to all students in their districts. We assume that in each of these California counties, many more children now have access to arts education than was the case before the Alliance for Arts Leadership and Arts for All were launched. Respondents in Boston claimed that the coordinated efforts in that city caused the number of OST slots for children to double over the previous several years, but these slots were not all for arts learning.

Despite access to arts learning experiences having increased and/or being on the increase in most of our sites at the time of our study, many children in these sites were yet to be served. There is no universal yardstick by which to objectively judge whether progress made in each site exceeded or fell short of expectations. However, we can say that universal access for all students in a given region, be it a city or a county, remained an unrealized goal for the sites studied. Site representatives stressed that they did not expect to achieve access for all without more years of work.

Even in the sites that were making strides in improving arts education access, arts education in the form of sequential stand-alone arts courses that are accessed by all students was rare in the schools. Of course, not all sites want these types of classes. The Alliance for Arts Learning Leadership, in Alameda County, prioritizes arts integration experiences for students. Big Thought, in Dallas, also orchestrates arts integration experiences, although it supports the development of sequential stand-alone courses, too. In Los Angeles County, school districts choose how they want to implement arts education programs. However, Arts for All coaches reported that most district plans prioritize arts integration because the schools lack the time and space needed for sequential stand-alone arts courses. Leaders of Arts for All concurred that "the how" of implementing sequential arts learning experiences in schools is much more difficult than convincing district leaders of the value of providing an arts education. One leader of this initiative commented as follows:

> We don't need more "why arts are important" videos. People in LA County value the arts and are interested in having the arts in schools. . . . We're at the "how."

---

[2]   The different models are discussed in Chapter Three in the section on Los Angeles County.

People are willing, but there are all the constraints, issues, and challenges. We in the field tend to get mushy when asked "how," and we instead start talking about "why." We need to be very specific about how to offer [the arts] when you have limited resources—not, here is how Einstein or Yo-Yo Ma thinks arts are important. The answer about the importance of the arts is not one research study away. We lack clear implementation strategies.

The district arts education leaders in both New York City and Chicago hope to develop sequential stand-alone arts courses through their systems. We did not, however, see or hear detailed plans indicating how this goal would be attained for all K–12 students.

Strategies to Improve Quality

Our impression from our case studies is that arts education leaders in each site are emphasizing access over quality. However, no individual or organization argued for greater access to "low-quality" programming. Indeed, various strategies have been employed to ensure or improve the quality of arts education provision in the sites.

We describe here the seven most commonly used strategies for improving the quality of arts learning experiences:[3]

1. strategic planning
2. requiring alignment with state standards
3. developing curriculum supports
4. building individual and organizational capacity
5. qualifying providers
6. coordinating peer review, ranking, and modeling
7. assessing student learning.

Strategic Planning

Strategic planning can help improve both access and quality. In some cases, strategic plans not only specify which students will be served when, but how programs will be evaluated and improved. In Alameda County, for example, the district-level plans submitted to the Alliance for Arts Learning Leadership as part of the MAP process must include strategies for assessing quality.

---

[3]   Two of these, strategic planning and capacity building, are strategies for improving access to arts learning experiences as well, as described earlier in this chapter.

Requiring Alignment with State Standards

Each of our sites was subject to arts education standards set by the state. These standards describe the content that should be covered in each grade level for the four common arts disciplines: music, dance, theater, and visual arts. The development of these standards has been applauded as an important step in defining a quality arts learning experience and providing concrete guidance to schools on arts program implementation. All of our sites made use of these standards to varying degrees.

The sites that relied heavily on external community-based providers—Alameda County, Los Angeles County, and Dallas—had mechanisms in place to ensure that programs were aligned with the standards. Arts for All, in Los Angeles County, offered annual training for community-based providers on how to align their programs with the standards. Providers applying to work with schools in these three sites were required to demonstrate how their programs met at least some of the standards. The programs were not expected to implement all of the standards, however.

School districts in our sites had policies requiring that teachers' curricula also align with the standards. The New York City Office of Arts and Special Projects took the standards a step further by developing the Blueprint curriculum guides. Teachers were expected to adhere to the Blueprints in their classrooms. In Dallas, we observed classrooms in which the state standards were up on the walls, and teachers described how they worked with them when designing lesson plans. Boston Public Schools had both state and local standards, and teachers received support from the district office to help them meet those standards. OST program providers in Boston were discussing the issue of state standards but at that time did not make use of them.

Developing Curriculum Supports

Teachers often desire supports that go beyond standards, such as curriculum frameworks and sample lesson plans. Several of our sites had developed such supports. New York City's Office of Arts and Special Projects had its Blueprints, which provide curricular guidance in the four arts disciplines. Interviewees in other sites referenced the Blueprints as models for curriculum support for teachers and external community-based providers. The Executive Director for the Fine Arts in the Dallas Independent School District reported that he and his team had expanded on the Dallas state standards by adding specificity, coherence, and rigor. This district had a curriculum writing process in which the state standards were built upon by creating curriculum planning guides describing how the particular knowledge or skill was to be taught, resources for instruction, assessments, and enrichment activities.

Arts for All staff members had developed an interactive Web site as another mechanism to promote quality through curriculum supports (Los Angeles County Arts Commission, 2008). This Web site, vetted by a panel of experts, was providing teachers and administrators with one-stop shopping for arts education programs that meet the California state content standards for visual and performing arts. It also offered models of arts education curriculum, policies, plans, and budgets; arts coordinator job descriptions; and survey, assessment, and strategic planning tools. In addition, there was a forum for sharing best practices and posing questions to the field.

Building Individual and Organizational Capacity

The building of classroom teacher, administrator, and artist capacity was described above as a strategy for improving access. It is also a strategy for improving quality. Interviewees reported that because the pipeline for certified arts specialists has deteriorated in many states, it is important to train teachers and artists to provide high-quality arts learning experiences. Training and support might be provided by district officials, such as the regional arts supervisors in the old New York City model, or by external providers working in concert with districts and schools. For example, in Dallas, ArtsPartners staff worked with teachers at each grade level in each elementary school twice a year, reviewing and discussing lesson plans.

Similarly, district and school administrators, as well as community-based providers, need support for their development and implementation of arts education plans. In Los Angeles County, Arts for All trained coaches to work with districts and schools, thereby ensuring a standard of quality for the coaches and jump-starting a cascading training process. The Alliance for Arts Learning Leadership did the same in Alameda County. And Arts for All's professional development program had trained about 400 local arts administrators and artists in dance, theater, music, and visual arts to incorporate the arts in the core curricula of school districts. In these programs, participants learned the fundamentals of child development, explored effective teaching and assessment strategies and varied learning styles, developed lesson plans and classroom management techniques, and learned to incorporate the arts within a variety of curriculum and interdisciplinary models.[4]

Qualifying Providers

In all of our sites, organizations external to the school district provided arts learning experiences in school and OST. Many of our interviewees thought that some of these cultural organizations and community-based providers did not always provide quality learning experiences. Their opinion was that these organizations survived because parents, teachers, and school administrators lack the knowledge and ability to distinguish between high- and low-quality learning experiences.

Some sites attempted to qualify community-based providers using both formal and informal qualification strategies. For example, Arts for All, in Los Angeles County, was building a sophisticated system for qualifying providers. Interested providers had to apply to be part of the Arts for All list and had to describe how their learning expe-

---

[4] The Los Angeles County Arts Commission provides descriptions of programs being offered (Los Angeles County Arts Commission, undated-b).

riences aligned with state standards. Applicants submitted streaming video of their arts learning experiences. Districts and schools then selected providers from those that passed this screening. In Dallas, providers become qualified to receive ArtsPartners (and therefore district) funding by demonstrating that their programs aligned with the Texas state arts education standards. Once in the system, providers' lesson plans were scored by a panel of school and peer reviewers. During this process, teachers learned more about curriculum and became more discerning about providers. Interviewees in Dallas reported that some external providers had, in fact, lost their contracts with schools as a result of this review and learning process. This ability to consider and measure providers side by side might not have emerged had ArtsPartners not made the effort to coordinate multiple organizations within one citywide arts education system.

Informally, the Alameda County Alliance for Arts Learning Leadership continued to refer the same set of external community-based providers to schools. The alliance refused to fund school and district arts education plans in cases where it doubted that the external partner would deliver a high-quality arts learning experience to students. The after-school office within the Chicago Public Schools was developing a list of providers, although it stopped short of claiming they were "qualified." In Boston, the mayor's office was vetting OST providers, and the Director of Arts Education had used a panel to help in this process. New York City had two lists of approved vendors for these types of services, one for in-school and one for OST programs.

Coordinating Peer Review, Ranking, and Modeling

Another strategy employed by our sites to improve quality was peer review, ranking, and modeling. Because quality criteria can be difficult to articulate and measure, peer review and interaction offer an alternative, effective approach. As one leader of the Arts for All movement in Los Angeles argued:

> It is difficult to describe in words what quality arts education is. People know quality when they see it. We try to expose principals to quality experiences so that they can get it. We're working on bringing board members out into schools too. Then light bulbs start going off; we're seeing it happen. We're creating more of those moments for superintendents/teachers to see it happen in a school like theirs. Not through a fancy speech in an auditorium. Peer-to-peer advocacy is the most effective strategy for spreading arts education. Superintendents are watching what other superintendents do. It spreads by word of mouth; it's peer to peer in terms of how it works. There are meetings on the calendar for this. We are also trying to piggyback on existing association conferences and meetings.

The process used by Dallas's ArtsPartners for colleagues to rank and discuss each other's lesson plans is an example of this strategy. In Alameda County, the Alliance for Arts Learning Leadership hosts summer institutes at which teachers and community-based providers share best practices. These institutes have become so popular that districts have vied to host them on their own campuses. An interviewee on the executive committee of Arts for All, in Los Angeles County, reported that he had fruitlessly argued the benefits of arts education with skeptics until he was blue in the face, but that these same skeptics became converts after observing high-quality arts education experiences in neighboring districts.

Assessing Student Learning

In all of our sites, individual teachers and program providers were assessing student learning through tests, portfolios, and performances. Boston Public Schools, with a grant from the Massachusetts Cultural Council, was developing voluntary arts assessments for each grade level and piloting them in a handful of schools. However, few sites were assessing student learning at the district (or community) level or even using course- or school-level assessment results for purposes other than providing grades in arts courses.

Tensions and Limitations Inherent in Strategies

The strategies used by the six sites to improve both access and quality are subject to their own tensions and limitations. This is not to say that these strategies are somehow wrong or will fail to achieve their goals, but, rather, that organizations implementing them should be aware of specific aspects of these strategies that could hamper progress or lead to unintended consequences.

High Standards Versus Highly Constrained Realities

Two of the six coordination efforts (Chicago and New York) were heavily focused on implementing in-school sequential, standards-based, stand-alone arts courses, and this goal was proving somewhat elusive. Several interviewees stressed that their state standards were overly ambitious and ultimately unattainable. The lack of time, space, and other resources within schools sounds like a well-worn and perhaps trite excuse, but it constitutes a real obstacle for arts educators. Although Los Angeles County's Arts for All hopes to encourage districts to provide at least some stand-alone arts courses, coaches reported that time and space limitations have almost always dictated that the arts be integrated into existing subjects. An Arts for All executive proclaimed that the "why" of establishing additional arts learning experiences is easy, but lamented frequently getting hung up on the "who, where, and how." Leaders of coordinated efforts in five sites were giving higher priority to in-school rather than OST arts learning opportunities. They defended this strategy by explaining that only a minority of students engaged in OST activities and not all of these activities were arts-learning related. However, all of the sites were having trouble fitting arts learning experiences into the school day. The OST providers we interviewed were frustrated by the lack of attention paid to the time available after school. They argued that more students could be attracted to arts learning experiences in OST through coordinated advocacy, funding, marketing to families, etc.

Capacity Lower Than Anticipated

Most sites viewed building individual teacher, artist, and principal capacity as one of their most important strategies. It can lead to further peer modeling and training and can help ensure that arts education remains in schools if community support dwindles and in communities if school supporters turn over. However, providers of capacity-building experiences were learning that turnovers occur all too frequently and that even those supporters that stay in place need more support than had been envisioned.

Los Angeles County's Arts for All, which had developed a model with two years of support, had many districts pleading to keep their coaches on after the two years. Some stand-alone providers, such as the Center for Community Partnerships in Chicago, had worked in the same schools for five to ten years. Given the lack of exposure to the arts in schools and of arts training in colleges of education, it is no surprise that administrators and teachers need support to provide arts education. Whether there are enough artists and arts educator coaches to provide this support is unknown, and the answer will vary according to the specifics of the local context. In most sites, the interviewees believed that the supply and quality of local artist educators were sufficient for current demand. But they were less certain about whether supply could meet plans for expansion. For example, respondents in Alameda County doubted the ability of external providers to expand much beyond the current levels of service.

Summary

We have now explored the strategies used in our six sites to build access to and improve the quality of arts learning experiences. Despite significant differences in the sites' approaches, eight strategies emerged as important in increasing access across the sites: auditing the state of arts education, setting a goal of access for all, strategic planning, constructing a case for why the arts matter, attracting and leveraging resources, hiring an arts education coordinator highly placed within the school district administration, building individual and organizational capacity, and engaging in advocacy. To improve quality, seven strategies were used across the sites: strategic planning; requiring alignment with state standards; developing curriculum supports; building individual and organizational capacity; qualifying providers; coordinating peer review, ranking, and modeling; assessing student learning. Examples of how the sites went about implementing these strategies were given. Communities interested in improving the quality of their arts learning experiences can review these approaches with an eye toward identifying those that fit their particular circumstances.

CHAPTER FIVE

Sparking and Sustaining Coordination Across Providers and Influencers

Chapter Four synthesized the strategies employed across the six study-case sites to improve both access to and quality of arts learning experiences for children. In this chapter, we consider the extent to which coordination of efforts accelerated and/or improved the effectiveness of these strategies in the six sites. We start by discussing coordination as an enabler of improved access and quality; we then turn to the conditions that fostered coordination and impeded it in our sites. We also provide observations about both the advantages and the drawbacks of participating in coordination efforts.

Coordination as an Enabler of Improved Access and Quality

Of the eight strategies adopted to improve access, three—conducting audits, setting a goal of access for all, and hiring an arts education coordinator highly placed within the school district administration—were in some cases adopted in the absence of coordination across organizations. However, any organization that sets a goal of serving all children (rather than just students in public schools) must involve different types of organizations in planning to achieve that goal. Another strategy—strategic planning—can be pursued without coordination but may be more likely to happen if an organization external to the district provides incentives. The other four strategies—constructing a case, building capacity, advocating, and attracting and leveraging resources—appear to be more successful when multiple organizations are coordinated within a region.

Because many schools and districts are isolated from one another, the strategy that seems to be the most bolstered by coordination among organizations outside the district is capacity building. Prior to these efforts, professional development opportunities were prevalent across our sites but not ubiquitous; and not all schools and districts were served by professional development providers in the arts, either through choice or because of ignorance about options. In addition, many members of district and school staffs had not been exposed to arts education when they were students and had not been trained to provide it as professionals. Therefore, any artist or teacher seeking professional development on his or her own was less likely to select appropriate providers and programs than an artist or teacher working within a network of people and organizations focused on identifying and supporting high-quality professional development opportunities. This strategy is facilitated by the existence of high-quality community-based providers within the relevant region, a condition met in each of our sites.

Based on our observations, strategies to improve quality seem to be strengthened by coordination. Strategies such as aligning provision with standards, developing curriculum supports, assessing student learning, qualifying providers, and strategic planning—all of these can be adopted by individual provider organizations. However, they all require knowledge and skills that not every provider possesses. Coordination among multiple organizations has the potential to overcome the knowledge and skill gaps that exist in any single provider organization, be it a school or non-school provider.

We found that coordination across organizations did lead to improved access to arts learning experiences, as well as other benefits, in some sites. However, we cannot say whether the coordinated efforts improved the quality of arts learning experiences. To date, there is little evidence that groups working together in a coordinated effort to improve access to arts learning have affected the quality of arts learning experiences, although there is evidence of strategies intending to improve quality.

Conditions That Foster Coordination

We found that the efforts of our six sites to coordinate across groups of providers and influencers prospered under specific conditions. What appear to foster coordination in the early stages are the convening of key stakeholders, effective leadership, and seed funding devoted specifically to coordination. In later stages, coordination is fostered through convening and joint planning, sustained funding, and evaluation, feedback, and improvement.

Convening of Key Stakeholders

In many of our sites, interviewees described early efforts to convene key stakeholders to discuss options for improving access to arts learning experiences. Conveners in these communities were usually one individual or organization, such as the County Arts Commission in Los Angeles County and the County Office of Education in Alameda County. The discussions were formal, planned public forums in some sites (e.g., Los Angeles County) and more-occasional meetings in others. Interviewees credited these early discussions with broadening support for arts education in the local community, overcoming ideological differences, laying groundwork for subsequent infrastructure for the coordination initiatives, and identifying local leadership talent.

Effective Leadership

Different studies note the importance of leadership in developing coordinated efforts to improve the provision of social services or education (e.g., Bodily et al., 2004; Dhuly, 1990; Keith, 1993; Stone, 1998; Tushnet, 1993; Mattessich and Monsey, 1992). We found that effective leaders share certain characteristics: They are capable, have an inclusive style, and are stable over time. In several cases, the leadership talent to manage and expand a collaborative effort grew over time as leaders became more experienced. In addition, collaborative leaders that came from outside the district were more effective at leading multi-organizational cooperative efforts than were leaders from inside the district (although Chicago's efforts in this regard are quite nascent).

Capable. In all of our study sites, at least one leader of the coordination efforts was recognized for his or her ability to offer legitimate leadership to the effort. Such leaders have legitimate convening power, stemming either from a professional title (as in Alameda County, where the leader works out of the Alameda County Office of Education) or from personal dedication and reputation (as in Chicago, where one leader of the early coordination efforts was on sabbatical from previous high-level positions). Based on their recognized knowledge and talents, these leaders are able to draw attention to the cause and recruit other individuals to commit to attending meetings and joining the coordination efforts. Most started as recognized authorities in either the arts or education, although some are best known for funding the arts or arts education.

Inclusive in style. A leader with an inclusive, non-pejorative style allows multiple organizations and individuals with differing views to feel welcome in the collaboration and to participate in finding creative ways to serve children in the community. In thinking about advice for other communities, one participant in the Los Angeles County initiative noted the following qualities as those of a good leader: "nimble," "fluid," and able to "seize moments," "understand diversity of those involved," and "be a learner as well as a leader." In several sites, but particularly in Alameda and Los Angeles counties and Dallas, interviewees felt that key leaders had non-judgmental, inclusive styles that not only welcomed other stakeholders to the table, but deliberately recruited them. These leaders were unifiers. By moving away from advocacy for a specific pedagogy, curriculum, or type of instructor, some were able to unite varied groups by their shared focus on aiding children and reducing social injustice. These leaders helped construct messages that gained widespread support and did not fall prey to arcane rivalries of the past. For example, leaders of Arts for All reported the following discussion on arts integration versus stand-alone arts courses:

> We debated [the issue] at great length during a planning process. [We were] split equally: 50/50. We tried to resolve it and come to a clear recommendation; but in the process, we realized that if [we were] that evenly split, we needed both. It was up to the district to decide; [there] wasn't a right or wrong answer. Elementary tended to be more integrated, but it was up to middle and high schools for arts

specialists to become more integrated. This was really a key moment when we said, "Okay, we need both. And that's okay! I can accept that." So everyone stopped fighting.

We note here that these leaders did not claim to have come to the job fully prepared with these sets of skills and talents. Several noted that they grew into the job as successes and failures honed their skills and abilities through sometimes difficult lessons learned.

Stable, dedicated to a long battle. Our interviewees stressed that leaders of coordination efforts must be stable, dedicated, and somewhat immune to setbacks. All pointed out that this work is never "done" and that advocating for arts education is an ongoing task. One interviewee even went so far as to say that leading efforts to advance arts education takes a special kind of person, one who is accustomed to being the underdog and fighting ongoing battles for recognition and legitimacy. Leaders of the coordination efforts in Dallas and in Los Angeles and Alameda counties were often described in these terms. These leaders frequently referred to their work as being on a ten- to 20-year timeline, or even as "endless." They articulated a deeply felt conviction that arts education would always need advocates and that their job would never be done. In addition, the cases showed the importance of stability over time in leading these efforts. The early turnover in Boston is an example of how an effort can founder when the leader leaves. The Dallas and Alameda sites are good examples of what can be accomplished when leaders remain in place over longer periods.

External to the school district. Some of our interviewees argued that school districts' central offices cannot effectively lead collaborative efforts and that leaders external to the district are thus essential. The central school system has strong incentives to focus on certain activities, particularly the improvement of mathematics and reading test scores, at the expense of other activities. There is growing evidence that this is indeed the case (Hamilton et al., 2007). McMurrer (2007) found that of 350 districts surveyed, 44 percent reported increasing the time spent on mathematics and reading by cutting an average of about 30 minutes per day from science, social studies, art, music, physical education, and recess. Furthermore, school district personnel are paid not to build external partnerships, but to ensure the functioning of the schools by hiring teachers, developing standards, and overseeing curriculum and instruction. District leaders of arts initiatives in our sample—in Boston, Chicago, and New York City—did just that.

Therefore, many took the view that there is much to be gained from leaders and other advocates for arts education being outside the district's central office structure. Only in this way could the full set of assets available in these arts-rich cities be brought to bear. Three of our case studies—Alameda County, Los Angeles County, and Dallas—show that leadership residing outside a central school district office was adept at involving multiple partners and influencers. Similarly, it was local foundations that spurred efforts in Chicago to hire a Director, Office of Arts Education, and in New York City to develop a plan for improving access. Our sample is, of course, too small for our findings to be conclusive, but they indicate that where leadership sits can be very important to whether a multi-organization collaboration emerges and whether that collaboration engages the assets available throughout the community.

Seed Funding for Coordination

Consistent with the three bodies of literature reviewed, all of the sites—even those whose efforts seemed to be emergent or even dissipating—noted that funds dedicated to coordination were crucial to getting these community-wide efforts off the ground. Leaders need to be compensated even if their salary is guaranteed for only a short period, and there must be funding for convening partners, conducting audits, analyzing the resultant data, and establishing strategic plans.

For our sites, initial seed funding came from different sources. In Dallas, the city and district each contributed $50,000 to found ArtsPartners. In Los Angeles County, Boston, Chicago, and New York City, foundations and other donors were key in supporting early efforts.

Coordination efforts in all of the sites were sparked by the receipt of funds dedicated to staff time and to coordinated activity planning. Whatever the need (for example, a staff position in the Alameda County Office of Education, or audits and a person dedicated to mapping the arts education networks in Boston), each community's efforts prospered when dedicated funds were available for coordination. Observers in these sites reported that funding for staff to enable coordination was a precious resource.

Convening and Joint Planning

In all of our sites, leaders with seed funding typically began by convening individuals and organizations for discussion, visioning, and planning sessions. In Los Angeles and Alameda counties and Dallas, these multiple group conversations allowed the leaders to tap others for the more-formal alliances and advisory groups. Leaders emerged from these informal conversations. Well-recognized structures then developed, enabling individuals to associate themselves via membership in an identifiable group having a mission, goals, and a set of strategies.

A grant award was often needed to get these activities off the ground (in New York City, for instance). According to our interviewees and the literature (Stone, 1998), the power to convene diverse groups and unite them in a joint planning effort is strongly correlated with leadership style and leaders' legitimacy as neutral advocates for improved access and quality rather than specific interventions.

Sustained Funding

The literature we reviewed notes that sustained funding is necessary for initiatives such as the coordinated efforts of our study. In all of the sites, sustained funding was needed to support the strategies and their implementation, as well as to provide incentives for schools and districts to join local initiatives and implement arts education programming. Then there are the efforts' leaders and staff members, all of whose salaries must be paid. Ideally, funds are also spent to evaluate the efforts, reflect on evaluation findings, and make concomitant improvements. Strategies for leveraging funding for this work are also essential. Funding in support of core coordination activities over and above the important work of developing and providing the programming in schools is an essential part of these community-wide efforts.

Evaluation, Feedback, and Improvement

A final fostering condition appears to be the inclusion of mechanisms for evaluation, feedback, and improvement to ensure that coordinated efforts are advancing toward established goals. Leaders in several sites clearly showed that they appreciate the value of these activities (and can put them in motion) for the coordination process and procedures, as well as their effects on arts education access and quality. Each site has taken some steps in the direction of evaluation and reflection. Leaders of Arts for All, in Los Angeles County, are in the process of making mid-course adjustments to better serve districts receiving new state funding for arts education. These leaders also monitor benchmarks for successful implementation of their Blueprints. Leaders of the Alliance for Arts Learning Leadership, in Alameda County, have hired an external evaluator to focus on the functioning of the alliance itself. In Dallas, Big Thought hired external evaluators to examine the effects of arts education on several student outcomes.

Conditions That Impede Coordination

Respondents who described their work in the coordination efforts in such terms as "never-ending" may be right. The histories of these sites provide evidence that arts education remains at best a stepchild in the curriculum and sometimes requires extraordinary efforts just to be kept in the family. Arts education will not achieve its full potential under conditions of fiscal constraint or social and economic inequities. Our interviewees pointed out many challenges to establishing coordinated efforts to improve access to arts learning experiences.

Changing Policy Contexts

Changing policy contexts emerged as a big challenge to coordination efforts.[1] All of the organizations leading these efforts exist within larger, state and local policy contexts. In New York City, the shift toward site-based management within the district necessitated a change in the course of coordination efforts there, which were to have been led

---

[1] Bodilly et al., 2004, presents similar findings.

by the central school district office. The enduring under-funding and reduced school hours in Chicago stand as testaments to the hostile infrastructure in which the arts seek to survive and thrive. The efforts in Dallas and the two California sites have been buoyed by the recent fiscal halcyon days. Similarly, the OST providers in Boston have benefited from significant fundraising. However, these beneficial supports can vanish with a change in administration. At the school level, they can be reversed by something as simple as a new principal who is not convinced that the arts are of benefit to students. Interviewees in Dallas and in Alameda and Los Angeles counties also stressed that new funding can bring its own challenges.

Conflict Among Providers and Ideas

Coordination efforts can be inhibited not just by the broader policy context, but also by philosophical and personality differences among organizational leaders. We learned of animosity between and within groups in every site. In some of the sites, the animosity stemmed from differing views about integration versus discipline-based approaches for arts education. Conflict based on this disagreement seemed to be the strongest in sites whose broad coordination efforts were the least advanced. As described above, leaders who can get beyond philosophical differences and achieve inclusion of different types of groups may be the most successful in advancing coordination. Expanding the school day or the resources for education as a whole may be one way to reduce the competition of ideas in some sites. When resources are in short supply, animosities and competition can increase.

Turnover in Leadership

Whereas lack of specific leadership talents has kept coordination efforts in some sites from prospering as expected, staff changes in key partner organizations and organizational changes in general have, according to respondents, posed ongoing challenges for coordination efforts. Careful agreements and deep understandings can be whisked away when key people move on. For those efforts that rely on supportive mayors to sustain them, such as the one in Boston, election of a new mayor may mean change, sometimes the disastrous kind. Looking forward, we expect that it will be challenging to maintain momentum in these local initiatives when their leaders leave. Given the extent to which the leaders of these efforts, particularly in Dallas and Los Angeles and Alameda counties, are recognized, respected, and deeply identified with the coordination efforts, they may be difficult to replace. The strategy in Los Angeles County to lead the initiative by committee may prove effective in that if one committee member turns over, the rest remain, not only to carry on the work, but also to assure funders and other stakeholders of continuity.

Advantages of Participating in Coordination Efforts

We found that coordination efforts offer some advantages to those who participate. Participants noted five in particular:

- *Some district and school officials reported that they appreciated the personal support gained by participating in coordinated efforts in their regions.* As discussed in Chapter Three, many districts throughout the United States have few arts teachers and administrators. Our interviewees reported feeling isolated as a supporter of arts education and unsure of how to access support for their own ideas and the generation of new ideas. For these individuals, broad coordination has provided much-appreciated support and guidance.
- *Some community-based providers and cultural organizations reported that their grant funding increased when they developed partnerships with districts and schools.* Given that many community-based providers are struggling to maintain their operations, expanded opportunities that lead to additional funding can ensure ongoing viability for some.
- *Funders reported satisfaction with their participation in system-building activities.* Funders in Los Angeles County explained that they would rather support Arts for All, in the hope that systemic change will result, than fund the same local schools individually each year to support arts programs likely to benefit only a few students. The members of the funding coalition led by The Chicago Community Trust are similarly hopeful that their support for the new Director, Office of Arts Education, will lead to systemic change.
- *Across the more coordinated sites, conversations about arts education are engaging diverse stakeholder groups—including small business owners, city council members, college officials, local foundation leaders, officials from city departments of parks and recreation, and corporate executives—and have led to additional funding, training programs, OST opportunities, and public support.*
- *Individuals leading coordination efforts reported being hopeful that their efforts will lead to systemic change, are proud of their accomplishments to date, and enjoy the work.* One leader of Los Angeles County's Arts for All reported that her involvement in this effort has been "the most rewarding aspect of my career." According to another leader, "It's been one of the most rewarding journeys I've been on. It's been difficult and challenging, but phenomenally rewarding." We do, of course, realize that enjoying one's work as a leader does not mean the work will have an impact; but satisfied leaders are likely to continue their work, thereby providing sustained leadership for these efforts. Several of the leaders in our sites have been promoting arts education for their entire careers and have been in the same leadership position for six to ten years.

Drawbacks of Participating in Coordination Efforts

We specifically asked our interviewees about the downside of participating in broad collaboration efforts. Although they did report drawbacks, they also reported that these were outweighed by the advantages. Similar to the findings of Bodilly et al.'s 2004 study of collaborative efforts to improve education, the drawbacks reported were as follows:

- time spent attending what seemed like endless meetings
- threats to funding of the individual organization posed by funding for the collaboration
- likelihood that some organizations were left out of the collaboration because of personal or political reasons
- artificial buy-in from schools and districts that are simply chasing incentive funding.

Some of the respondents also mentioned a related item: the difficulty of discussing arts education in groups consisting of members of diverse organizations, many of whom are unfamiliar with the particular lingo.

Summary

We identified certain conditions that foster coordination. To begin with, the most important conditions are effective leadership and seed funding. In sites where these two conditions were met, providers and influencers were able to have the conversations needed to propel the efforts forward, resulting in formal structures of leadership and advisory groups. Continued funding of these structures is another condition that must be met, as is that of evaluation, feedback, and improvement.

Unfortunately, the two sparking conditions, effective leadership and seed funding, may be hard to find in the sites that would like to achieve more-effective and more-efficient coordination across providers and influencers. The specific styles and attributes of the effective leaders in several of our sites appear to be particularly non-replicable, lending some credence to the argument that successful community efforts are unique to themselves. However, seed funding, if it can be found, might help identify or develop such leaders. Other conditions that foster coordination should be easier for sites to adopt—for example, convening and joint planning, and evaluation, feedback, and improvement.

For most of our respondents, broad coordination of individuals and organizations across regions to increase access for children to arts learning experiences appears to be beneficial, which is an encouraging message for other communities. However, an important condition that impedes coordination efforts—shifts in the policy context that slow or derail cooperative efforts—comes into play everywhere. In consequence, long-term coordination efforts may be a necessity as long as the prevailing education context devalues arts learning compared with other forms of learning.

CHAPTER SIX

Conclusions

In this chapter, we gather and present our findings and offer guidance, in the form of recommendations, for communities attempting to improve access to quality arts learning experiences for children. We end the chapter with an important message about the power, and the fragility, of coordinated efforts aimed at improving access to high-quality arts education.

Findings

Ecology of Local Arts Education

In conducting this work, we learned that the arts education ecology comprises multiple providers of and influencers of arts education. Some of these advocate for specific approaches to arts learning and its provision (which leads to entrenched disagreements); others search for commonalities. In general, we found the arts education field to have a rich, multifaceted view of arts education's goals and of what "quality" provision implies. Moreover, our investigation confirmed the view that the arts struggle to keep a foothold in the urban school curriculum because of such factors as lack of space in the schools and lack of time in the school day, as well as the greater value being placed on other subjects. The state arts education standards are indeed significant steps forward in providing arts education guidance to practitioners, but they have not been met in the sites we investigated. Both our study and recent surveys attest to the fact that access to arts learning experiences in public schools appears to be uneven and idiosyncratic.

Through interviews of experts, literature reviews, and case studies, we uncovered four groups of arts education providers, some relatively new and some more mature: schools, cultural organizations, community-based providers, and OST providers. Much of the literature on arts education and most of the reforms have focused on schools, but fiscal crises and community reactions over the past few decades have led to a more complex arts education ecology, one in which many non-school entities have launched and refined their own provision of arts learning experiences. All four provider groups are influenced by an array of arts education policies and practices—from higher education institutions, city and state governments, school districts, and philanthropic interests—that are diffuse and often weak because the needed resources are lacking. In short, the system of arts education provision that has evolved is highly complex and as yet has been unable to reverse the dismantling of arts learning in the nation's urban public schools.

Coordinated Community Approaches to Improving Access

In each of the six sites, many types of providers offer arts learning experiences for children both in and outside of school on an independent basis. Our focus was specifically on initiatives to coordinate multiple organizations in pursuit of improved arts learning, however, so we acknowledge these other types of efforts but note that we did not address or consider them in our investigation.

We identified four different patterns of coordination across providers and groups in the six case studies, each influenced by local context and history. The Alameda County and Los Angeles County efforts primarily focused on in-school provision but sought to work closely with non-school providers. These efforts were guided by county-level agencies. Boston's effort focused on coordination among OST providers and was led by newly formed community-based organizations and the mayor's office. Arts learning in this case was not central to the coordination efforts except as supported by a handful of foundations and, very recently, a small office within the broader mayor's office. Chicago and New York City's efforts focused on in-school, stand-alone, sequenced courses and entailed only modest coordination across providers and influencers. Dallas's effort focused on both in-school and OST delivery through stand-alone courses and integrated curriculum. Its efforts were broad, involving all types of providers throughout the community.

The motivations for establishing the coordinated efforts varied but often stemmed from leaders' long-standing, deep dissatisfaction with the lack of systemic access to arts learning experiences in their communities. These leaders came to believe that the best way to improve access to arts education was to join forces. By bringing together multiple organizations, all with the goal of improving access to high-quality arts learning experiences, it would be possible to compete against the political and structural focus on subjects other than the arts, to better leverage resources, and to overcome inequities in provision within the community.

Strategies Used to Improve Access and Quality

The sites used a multitude of strategies to promote access: conducting audits of arts education, setting a goal of access for all, strategic planning, constructing a case, attracting and leveraging resources, hiring an arts education coordinator highly placed within the school district administration, building individual and organizational capacity, and advocating. Sites also used strategies to improve quality: strategic planning; requiring alignment with state standards; developing curriculum supports; building individual and organizational capacity; qualifying providers; coordinating peer review, ranking, and modeling; and assessing student learning. Some of these strategies, such as building individual capacity, advocating, attracting and leveraging resources, qualifying providers, and coordinating peer review activities, are more likely to flourish when organizations work in coordination with each other using the assets and expertise across the community to improve. Other strategies, however, appear to be useful regardless of whether organizations work together.

Strategies to Spark and Sustain Coordination

Case histories have demonstrated that effective leadership is necessary for coordination efforts to progress. In several of our case studies that saw considerable progress, leaders showed an inclusive style, supporting multiple approaches to pedagogy and achieving the involvement of multiple and diverse groups. In two cases, efforts involving primarily school districts ignored the possibly important contributions of the community's large and healthy sector of non-school providers. Early seed funding specifically for the coordination function proved crucial to coordination. This seed funding allowed sites to develop coordinating bodies and pay for positions for those (especially leaders) who could convene the different groups or perform community audits to understand the extent of current provision and identify significant gaps. Moreover, dialog among those convened could lead to formal structures for collaboration and further joint planning.

Challenges to Coordinated Efforts

The greatest challenge to the coordinated efforts in the sites was rapid shifts in policy. The New York City case is a clear example of how a shift in policy, this one by the New York City Department of Education's chancellor, can impact efforts at collaboration around arts education. Changes in leadership and inconsistent support over the long term can also have deleterious effects that slow efforts; what happened to the early efforts in Boston is an example of this issue.

Other challenges are less obvious or are so obvious that they are easily overlooked. For example, because leaders of the coordinated efforts we studied tended to target the most willing districts and schools by encouraging schools to respond to incentives, there have not yet been concerted efforts to convert the uninterested. This is particularly problematic where site-based management exists, because in this case the district-level levers for change are less influential. Where site-based management is in force, principals will have to be persuaded of the value of arts education one by one—a challenging task mainly because of the time involved and the frequency of principal turnover.

The lack of time, space, and other resources within schools and OST programs may seem like a well-worn and perhaps trite excuse for children's lack of access to arts education, but these barriers are a real and constant obstacle. They impede the goal at many sites of providing in-school access (especially to sequential stand-alone courses) and increasing access to OST activities. What is often overlooked is that this lack of time, space, and other resources for arts education is the result of policy, which can be changed. Obviously, the Dallas and the Los Angeles and Alameda county cases stand as examples of how local policy can be changed to bring more resources to arts programs.

Other challenges have only recently become evident. Some argue, for instance, that arts education is important in the schools because the arts help improve student learning in other subjects, as measured on test scores. This argument could backfire if expected improvements do not occur. While we hope this does not happen, it might be prudent to stress the association of arts learning with important intrinsic and youth development benefits that the growing collaborative efforts could measure and document, rather than to rest one's case solely on the benefits of the arts to learning in other subjects.

Finally, providers of capacity-building experiences in the arts education field have begun to learn that staff turnovers occur all too frequently and that even staff members who stay need more support than was envisioned. Thus, as these efforts become more successful, they face more, rather than fewer, demands for resources—especially for people and expertise, which are the more difficult resources to develop in the short run.

Guidance for Practitioners

The confines of our study limited us to capturing the efforts of only six sites, all urban, at a single point in time, which means our findings may not be easily transferred to other communities. With this caveat, we offer what we see as the most useful insights for other communities to consider. Those wishing to extract potential lessons should view these recommendations in light of their own situations.

Recommendations for Improving Coordination and Access to Quality Arts Learning Experiences

Some of the factors that foster coordination may be difficult to replicate in other sites. This is especially true of effective leadership, which is an important fostering factor. However, seed funding, accompanied by sustained interest by foundations or community leaders, could bring forth the capable, inclusive in style, and stable leaders needed. Several of the collaborative leaders we interviewed noted how their skills and expertise developed over time and with support. Seed funding and some initial collaborative talent can be mutually reinforcing factors that support leadership development.

The case-study sites differed enough from each other to demonstrate that coordination efforts sprout and develop according to a community's specific circumstances, including its available funding and leadership assets. The fact that a county arts commission took the lead in one of our sites while a county office of education did so in another suggests that more than one approach can bear fruit. Although our interviewees noted the importance of position-based legitimacy for leaders of coordination efforts, most communities have multiple organizations that could lead coordination efforts. Where to start such an effort depends partly on where the willing and capable leaders reside. In many of our sites, leaders felt somewhat reluctant in the early years of the local initiative; they questioned whether broad coordination efforts were truly a legitimate role for them and their organizations. But their dedication and commitment to improving access to arts education for children outweighed their reservations.

These cases also provide specific examples of strategies that could be used to improve both access to and quality of arts education, not least of which is the use of initial audits or maps of the current state of arts learning provision. Using these data to establish a jointly agreed-upon goal of access for all may be a key strategy. Achieving access for all is more likely when multiple organizations set this goal and work together to obtain it. Our interviewees reported that prior to the collective efforts, they had hoped that access for all would occur naturally through advocacy campaigns and increased funding of community-based providers. They then realized that these strategies were limited and that a more promising approach was to set clear goals of access for all and develop strategic plans for achieving those goals. The Dallas site was the most successful in using coordinated effort to create synergy between the school sector and non-school providers to improve access to arts learning activities. It was also the site with the longest-running history of coordination.

Many sites deliberately combined several strategies, especially in their attempts to improve access. Alameda and Los Angeles counties and Dallas, for example, conducted audits, set a goal of access for all, developed strategic plans, made a case for arts education, and advocated for the arts. According to our respondents, these activities complement each other well and are more powerful in combination than in isolation. The sites that implemented combined strategies were also fairly successful in attracting resources.

The importance of individual capacity and talent and of concrete policy and practical supports also showed in our case studies. In the arts education field, with its "missing generation" of citizens who were not exposed to arts education as students or in their professional lives, the task of developing individual capacity appears to be crucial. Thus, individuals and organizations in our sites focused on providing professional development, building networks, strengthening leaders, developing advocacy strategies, and the like. As with education in general (McDonnell and Elmore, 1987; McLoughlin, 1990; Fullan, 1999), improving access and instruction is as heavily intertwined with human resource and community-building efforts and embedding capacity and advocacy in people as it is with developing standards and curriculum and building structures such as transportation to programs. Programs can be cut in times of fiscal crisis, but people with the right talents, skills, and interests can sustain efforts through difficult times. Arts teachers who are laid off in funding crises can resurface within community-based providers, or as general education teachers, or as citizen advocates pressing for the renewal of arts education. Community leaders should give careful consideration to the need to develop resilient and sustainable practices, ones that are ultimately embedded in the changed values and improved skills of advocates, educators, and education leaders.

Because individuals with talents in arts and education can be found both in and outside of school, it seems appropriate and important to recognize the assets that exist across the community. If, as our study indicates, arts education's standing is relatively weak in relation to that of other disciplines, those most interested in promoting arts education need as many as possible of these assets at their disposal to move forward against the tide of competing interests. Fragmentation of the arts education field into separate and often vying groups based on pedagogy and curriculum or excessive focus on one class of provider to the exclusion of others seems ill advised in a sector that is weak compared with its competitors for time and space in the lives of children. Philanthropies, community leaders, and the leaders of provider organizations would do well to minimize the vocal differences among these groups and maximize the united front needed to successfully promote arts education. Indeed, many of our interviewees stressed the need to replace the divisive arguments over arts integration versus discipline-based stand-alone arts courses with the acknowledgment that both are needed. A unified front would knock down one major obstacle and form a combined voice for tackling those remaining, such as test-based accountability's focus on non-arts subjects and limited time in the school day.

By calling for reconciliation, we are not implying a need for uniformity. The differences represent important aspects of the ecology that must be considered. Leaders of coordinated efforts could provide a valuable service to their communities by carefully thinking about and then clearly articulating what they mean by access and how they want to measure it, and then mapping goals for improved access. Careful thought must also be given to what is meant by quality of provision and how to assess quality, something that was just beginning to take place in the sites we studied.

Finally, district, school, and community leaders need specific guidance on how to offer arts education given limited resources. Currently, the field as a whole lacks clear strategies for implementing high-quality programming for all children.

Recommendations for Monitoring Progress

Communities that set out to develop coordinated efforts aimed at improving children's access to quality arts learning experiences will want to measure their progress. Based on the findings of our study, the following indicators of progress may be useful for the task:

- commitment to a mutual goal—to improving access, quality, or both
- leadership that bridges divides
- distributed leadership; stability through changes in leadership
- shared information about the field, activities, best practices, etc.
- jointly developed and implemented policies, structures, and activities
- pooled resources
- positive policy and funding trends
- development of feedback loops and concomitant improvements.

Communities attempting to improve access to and the quality of children's arts learning experiences through coordinated efforts will also want to measure whether they are achieving these outcomes for children. Our sites measured access in different ways: number of students enrolling in arts education courses, ratio of arts specialists to students, number of youth served in OST programs, number of districts and schools developing and implementing arts education plans, etc. But no site measured access longitudinally across all providers to get a true sense of the level of access across a site or the progress made over time.

Our sites' attempts to measure the quality of arts learning experiences were far fewer. Leaders of the Office of Arts and Special Projects in New York City hoped to begin evaluating the quality of programs in the city's public school system in the future. Leaders of other efforts had implemented several strategies to improve quality, such as establishing the expectation and understanding that districts will develop their own evaluation mechanisms and will be held accountable for their progress.

The current and ongoing work of Harvard's Project Zero on the qualities of quality suggests that provision of quality arts experiences has several layers to it: Certain actors are responsible for ensuring that the conditions for quality exist, while the core of the experience is the engagement of the child and teacher (be it an artist or an arts specialist).[1] Therefore, evaluations could be multilayered as well, determining that the conditions are available for a high-quality learning experience and then focusing on the quality of that experience itself.

A Sometimes Powerful, but Also Fragile Approach

According to our study, cities and counties in which there are efforts to coordinate providers and influencers in order to improve access to arts education appear to be making headway against the long-standing devaluing of arts education in the public schools. In all cases, however, we found these efforts to be fragile, vulnerable not only to policy and political changes, but also to blows such as test-based assessments of non-arts subjects

---

[1] Project Zero reports are available (as of September 9, 2007) at its Web site: http://www.pz.harvard.edu.

and the related lack of time and space in the school day for other than tested subjects. The so-called missing generation of teachers and school leaders who have not been exposed to arts education, either as students or as professionals, adds to the fragility.

Current efforts are resulting in improved access to arts learning experiences primarily in the schools and sometimes in communities. We do not know whether these experiences are of high quality, however. As discussed throughout this report, the meaning of "quality programming" and the definition of its manifestation differ from provider organization to provider organization, and sometimes from person to person, making consensus on a shared goal of quality more difficult to achieve initially than consensus on a shared goal of access. The fact that the sites we studied are using strategies to improve quality is promising, but the fruits of these efforts have not yet been systematically evaluated.

More than anything else, our analysis emphasizes the existence of a rich, complex, and yet delicate ecology in these communities, where shifting policy and enthusiasm are the norm. Those working to improve access to arts learning experiences must navigate churning waters. But in at least several cases, coordination efforts have produced a powerful vehicle for change, a vehicle missing in other communities. Unfortunately, a coordination effort that is poorly situated within the community, narrow in its recognition of assets or partners, or planted within an organization subject to overnight policy shifts can be quite fragile. Insights from our study should give some hope to those engaged in the work of elevating the stature of arts education. It is best that they take nothing for granted and remain guardedly optimistic that their efforts, if well planned and executed, will eventually give more children opportunities to engage in high-quality arts learning experiences.

References

Arts, Education, and Americans Panel. *Coming to Our Senses: The Significance of the Arts for American Education.* New York: McGraw Hill, 1977.

Arts Education Partnership. *The Arts and Education: New Opportunities for Research.* Washington, D.C.: Arts Education Partnership, 2004. As of December 31, 2007:
http://www.aep-arts.org/files/publications/OpportunitiesResearch.pdf

Arts Education Partnership, American Arts Alliance, American Association of Museums, American Symphony Orchestra League, Americans for the Arts, Association of Art Museum Directors, Association of Performing Arts Presenters, Dance/USA, The John F. Kennedy Center for the Performing Arts/Kennedy Center Alliance for Arts Education Network, MENC: The National Association for Music Education, National Assembly of State Arts Agencies, OPERA America, Theatre Communications Group, VSA arts. *No Subject Left Behind: A Guide to Arts Education Opportunities in the 2001 NCLB Act.* Washington, D.C.: Arts Education Partnership, 2004.

Arts Education Partnership National Forum. *Creating Quality Integrated and Interdisciplinary Arts Programs.* Washington, D.C.: Arts Education Partnership, September 2002.

Associated Press. "State Sees Drop in the Number of Arts Teachers," July 24, 2005. As of January 1, 2008:
http://www.capitalnews9.com/content/top_stories/?ArID=141670

Banathy, Bela H., and Patrick M. Jenlink. "Systems Inquiry and Its Application in Education," in David H. Jonassen, ed., *Handbook of Research on Educational Communications and Technology*, 2nd ed. Mahwah, N.J.: Lawrence Erlbaum Associates, Inc., 2004.

Bergoni, Louis, and Julia Smith. *Effects of Arts Education on Participation in the Arts, Executive Summary.* Washington, D.C.: National Education Association, 1996.

Bodilly, Susan J., and Megan K. Beckett. *Making Out-of-School-Time Matter: Evidence for an Action Agenda.* Santa Monica, Calif.: RAND Corporation, 2005. As of December 30, 2007:
http://www.rand.org/pubs/monographs/MG242/

Bodilly, Susan J., Joan Chun, Gina S. Ikemoto, and Sue Stockly. *Challenges and Potential of a Collaborative Approach to Education Reform.* Santa Monica, Calif.: RAND Corporation, 2004. As of December 30, 2007:
http://www.rand.org/pubs/monographs/MG216/

Boston After School and Beyond. Web page, "Our History," undated. As of January 1, 2008:
http://www.bostonbeyond.org/aboutus/our-history.html

Boston Public Schools. Web site at-a-glance section, undated. As of January 1, 2008:
http://boston.k12.ma.us/bps/bpsglance.asp

Burnaford, Gail, Arnold Aprill, and Cynthia Weiss, eds. *Renaissance in the Classroom: Arts Integration and Meaningful Learning.* Mahwah, N.J.: Lawrence Erlbaum Associates, 2001.

CAE—*see* Center for Arts Education

California Arts Council. *Current Research in Arts Education: An Arts in Education Research Compendium.* Sacramento, Calif.: California Arts Council, 2001. As of December 31, 2007:
http://www.cac.ca.gov/86

California Department of Education. Funding and Grants Web page, "Arts and Music Block Grant," Funding Profile (ID 953), last modified May 7, 2007. As of January 1, 2008:
http://www.cde.ca.gov/fg/fo/profile.asp?id=953

California Food Policy Advocates. *Alameda County: A Profile of Poverty, Hunger and Food Assistance.* San Francisco, Calif.: California Food Policy Advocates, June 2002. As of January 1, 2008:
http://www.dhs.ca.gov/ps/cdic/cpns/research/download/appendix/Alameda.pdf

Center for Arts Education. *A Decade of Progress.* New York: Center for Arts Education, 2007.

Chapman, Laura. "Coming to Our Senses: Beyond the Rhetoric," *Art Education*, 31(1), January 1978.

—————. *Instant Art, Instant Culture: The Unspoken Policy for American Schools.* New York: Teachers College Press, 1982.

—————. "Arts Education as a Political Issue: The Federal Legacy," in Ralph A. Smith and Ronald Berman, eds., *Public Policy and the Aesthetic Interest.* Champaign, Ill.: University of Illinois Press, 1992, pp. 119–136.

Chicago Public Schools. Web site at-a-glance section, undated. As of January 1, 2008:
http://www.cps.k12.il.us/AtAGlance.html

Consortium of National Arts Education Associations. *Authentic Connections: Interdisciplinary Work in the Arts*, 2002. As of January 1, 2008:
http://www.naea-reston.org/pdf/INTERart.pdf

Csikszentmihalyi, Mihaly. *Creativity: Flow and the Psychology of Discovery and Invention.* New York: Harper Perennial, 1996.

Davidson, Benjamin, and Lisa Michener. *National Arts Education Public Awareness Campaign Survey.* Washington, D.C.: Americans for the Arts, July 1, 2001.

Day, Michael, Elliot W. Eisner, Robert Stake, Brent Wilson, Marjorie Wilson, Milbrey Wallin McLaughlin, and Margaret Ann Thomas. *Art History, Art Criticism, and Art Production: An Examination of Art Education in Selected School Districts, Volume II: Case Studies of Seven Selected Sites.* Santa Monica, Calif.: RAND Corporation, 1984. As of January 9, 2008:
http://www.rand.org/pubs/reports/R3161.2/

Deasy, Richard J., ed. *Critical Links: Learning in the Arts and Student Academic and Social Development.* Washington, D.C.: Arts Education Partnership, 2002.

Delacruz, Elizabeth Manley, and Phillip C. Dunn. "The Evolution of Discipline-Based Art Education," *Journal of Aesthetic Education*, 30(3), Autumn 1996.

Dluhy, Milan J. *Building Coalitions in the Human Services.* Newbury Park, Calif.: Sage Publications, 1990.

Donaldson, Lynn, and Erika Pearsall. *Arts Education in the Chicago Public Schools.* Chicago, Ill.: Chicago Community Trust, 2002.

Dreeszen, Craig. *Trends in Arts Education Collaborations*. 2001 Fowler Colloquium Papers at the University of Maryland. As of December 31, 2007:
http://www.lib.umd.edu/PAL/SCPA/fowlercolloq2001paper1.html

Dreeszen, Craig, Arnold Aprill, and Richard Deasy. *Learning Partnerships: Improving Learning in Schools with Arts Partners in the Community*. Washington, D.C.: Arts Education Partnership, 1999. As of January 17, 2008:
http://www.aep-arts.org/files/publications/LearningPartnerships.pdf

Education Commission of the States. "State Policies Regarding Arts in Education," *ECS StateNotes: Arts in Education*, November 2005. As of January 1, 2008:
http://www.ecs.org/clearinghouse/63/92/6392.doc

Eisner, Elliot W., "The State of Art Education Today and Some Potential Remedies: A Report to the National Endowment for the Arts," *Art Education*, 31(8), December 1978.

——————. "Does Experience in the Arts Boost Academic Achievement?" *Arts Education Policy Review*, 100(1), September–October 1998.

Fiske, Edward B., ed. *Champions of Change: The Impact of the Arts on Learning*. Washington, D.C.: The Arts Education Partnership and the President's Committee on the Arts and the Humanities, 1999. As of December 30, 2007:
http://artsedge.kennedy-center.org/champions/pdfs/ChampsReport.pdf

Fullan, Michael. *Change Forces: The Sequel*. London: Falmer Press, 1999.

Gardner, Howard. "Zero-Based Arts Education: An Introduction to Arts PROPEL," *Studies in Art Education*, 30(2), Winter 1989.

Greene, M. *Variations on a Blue Guitar: The Lincoln Center Lectures on Aesthetic Education*. New York: Teachers College, 2001.

Guthrie, Julian, and Jesse Hamlin. "Schools Short on Fine-Arts Teachers: Districts Get Creative to Take up the Slack," *San Francisco Chronicle*, May 15, 2002. As of January 1, 2008:
http://www.sfgate.com/cgi-bin/article.cgi?f=/c/a/2002/05/15/DD200607.DTL

Hamilton, Laura S., Brian M. Stecher, Julie A. Marsh, Jennifer Sloan McCombs, Abby Robyn, Jennifer Russell, Scott Naftel, and Heather Barney. *Standards-Based Accountability Under No Child Left Behind: Experiences of Teachers and Administrators in Three States*. Santa Monica, Calif.: RAND Corporation, 2007. As of December 30, 2007:
http://www.rand.org/pubs/monographs/MG589/

Harris, Louis. *Americans and the Arts: Highlights from a Nationwide Survey of the Attitudes of the American People Toward the Arts*. Prepared for the American Council for the Arts. Scholastic Inc., June 1996.

Heath, Shirley Brice, Elisabeth Soep, and Adelma Roach. "Living the Arts Through Language and Learning: A Report on Community-Based Youth Organizations," *Americans for the Arts Monographs*, 2(7), November 1998, pp. 1–20.

Herbert, Douglas. "Finding the Will and the Way to Make the Arts a Core Subject: Thirty Years of Mixed Progress," *The State Education Standard*, 4(4), Winter 2004. As of January 17, 2008:
http://www.nasbe.org/Standard/15_Winter2004/Herbert.pdf

Keith, Joanne. *Building and Maintaining Community Coalitions on Behalf of Children, Youth and Families*. Project Report, Community Coalitions in Action, Institute for Children, Youth and Families. East Lansing, Michigan: National Network for Collaboration, 1993. As of December 30, 2007:
http://crs.uvm.edu/nnco/collab/buildcoal1.html

Longley, Laura, ed. *Gaining the Arts Advantage.* Washington, D.C.: The Arts Education Partnership and the President's Committee on the Arts and Humanities, 1999.

Los Angeles County Arts Commission. Web page, "Arts Education: Arts for All," undated-a. As of January 1, 2008:
http://lacountyarts.org/artseducation.html

——————. Arts Education: Arts for All Web page, "Artist Training," undated-b. As of January 1, 2008:
http://lacountyarts.co.la.ca.us/artsed/artsed_profdev.html

——————. *Arts for All: Los Angeles County Regional Blueprint for Arts Education.* Los Angeles, Calif.: Los Angeles County Arts Commission, September 2002. As of January 1, 2008:
http://www.lacountyarts.org/artsed/docs/artsedu_artsforall09-02.pdf

——————. Web site, "Arts for All: Resources for Schools and Communities," 2008. As of January 1, 2008:
http://tools.laartsed.org/default.aspx

Mattessich, Paul W., and Barbara R. Monsey. *Collaboration: What Makes It Work—A Review of Research Literature on Factors Influencing Successful Collaboration.* St. Paul, Minn.: Amherst Wilder Foundation, 1992.

McCarthy, Kevin F., Elizabeth H. Ondaatje, Laura Zakaras, and Arthur Brooks. *Gifts of the Muse: Reframing the Debate About the Benefits of the Arts.* Santa Monica, Calif.: RAND Corporation, 2004. As of January 1, 2008:
http://www.rand.org/pubs/monographs/MG218/

McDonnell, Lorraine M., and Richard F. Elmore. *Alternative Policy Instruments.* Santa Monica, Calif.: RAND Corporation, 1987. As of January 1, 2008:
http://www.rand.org/pubs/joint_notes-education/JNE03/

McLoughlin, Milbrey. "The RAND Change Agent Study Revisted: Macro Perspectives and Micro Realities," *Education Researcher*, 19(9), December 1990.

McMurrer, Jennifer. *Choices, Changes, and Challenges: Curriculum and Instruction in the NCLB Era.* Washington, D.C.: Center on Education Policy, July 24, 2007.

Mezzacappa, Dave. "Full-Time Art, Music Teachers: A Dwindling Breed?" *Philadelphia Public School Notebook*, Summer 2006. As of January 1, 2008:
http://www.thenotebook.org/editions/2006/summer/fulltime01.htm

Museums Without Walls. *Arts in Focus: Los Angeles Countywide Arts Education Survey.* Los Angeles, Calif.: Los Angeles County Arts Commission, 2001. As of January 1, 2008:
http://www.lacountyarts.org/artsed/docs/AIFMay01.pdf

Music for All Foundation. *The Sound of Silence. The Unprecedented Decline of Music Education in California Public Schools: A Statistical Review.* Warren, N.J.: Music for All Foundation, September 2004.

National Center for Education Statistics. "The NAEP 1997 Arts Education Assessment: An Overview," *Focus on NAEP*, 2(4), August 1998.

——————. *Arts Education in Public Elementary and Secondary Schools: 1999–2000.* Washington, D.C.: U.S. Department of Education, May 2002a.

—————. "Characteristics of the 100 Largest Public Elementary and Secondary School Districts in the United States: 2000–2001," Table 9. U.S. Department of Education, 2002b. As of January 1, 2008:
http://nces.ed.gov/pubs2002/100_largest/table_09_1.asp

National Commission on Excellence in Education. *A Nation at Risk: The Imperative of Education Reform*. An Open Letter to the American People; A Report to the Nation and the Secretary of Education, United States Department of Education. Washington, D.C., April 1983. As of December 31, 2007:
http://www.ed.gov/pubs/NatAtRisk/index.html

National Endowment for the Arts. *Toward Civilization: A Report on Arts Education*. Washington, D.C.: National Endowment for the Arts, 1988.

NCES—*see* National Center for Education Statistics

NEA—*see* National Endowment for the Arts

New York City Arts in Education Roundtable. Press release. "Annual Report Shows Continuing Financial Support by Cultural Organizations for School Programs: Attests to Commitment of the Cultural Community to Arts in the Schools," May 5, 2006. Available at:
http://www.nycaieroundtable.org/docs/0405SurveyPressRelease.doc

New York City Department of Education. *Blueprint for Teaching and Learning in the Arts Grades K-12*, New York: New York City Department of Education, 2004.

New York State Board of Regents. Press release. "506 Title I Schools and 56 Districts Statewide Are 'In Need of Improvement' Under NCLB; 193 Schools Also Identified Under Separate State Rules." Albany, New York: University of the State of New York, January 10, 2007. As of January 1, 2008:
http://www.oms.nysed.gov/press/sini11007.htm

No Child Left Behind Act—*see* Public Law 107-110

Ohio Arts Council. *Ohio: A State for the Arts. State of the Arts Report*. 2001. As of January 1, 2008:
http://www.ohiosoar.org/intro/

Oreck, Barry. "The Artistic and Professional Development of Teachers: A Study of Teachers' Attitudes Toward and Use of the Arts in Teaching," *Journal of Teacher Education*, 55(1), 2004.

Pogrebin, Robin. "Renewed Push for the Artistic ABC's in N.Y.," *The New York Times*, June 26, 2006. As of December 27, 2007:
http://www.travel.nytimes.com/2006/06/26/arts/26blue.html

Public Law 107-110. No Child Left Behind Act of 2001, January 8, 2002.

Rabkin, Nick, and Robin Redmond, eds. *Putting the Arts in the Picture: Reframing Education in the 21st Century*. Chicago, Ill.: Columbia College Chicago, 2004.

Remer, Jane. *Changing Schools Through the Arts: How to Build on the Power of an Idea*. Rev. ed. Washington, D.C.: Americans for the Arts, January 1, 1990.

—————. *Beyond Enrichment: Building Effective Arts Partnerships with Schools and Your Community*. Washington, D.C.: Americans for the Arts, May 1, 1996.

Rowe, Melissa, Laura Werber Castaneda, Tessa Kaganoff, and Abby Robyn. *Arts Education Partnerships: Lessons Learned from One School District's Experience*. Santa Monica, Calif.: RAND Corporation, 2004. As of December 30, 2007:
http://www.rand.org/pubs/monographs/MG222/

Ruppert, Sandra S., and Andrew L. Nelson. *From Anecdote to Evidence: Assessing the Status and Condition of Arts Education at the State Level.* Washington, D.C.: Arts Education Partnership, November 2006.

Seidel, Steve, Meredith Eppel, and Maria Martiniello. *Arts Survive: A Study of Sustainability in Arts Education Partnerships.* Cambridge, Mass.: Project Zero at Harvard Graduate School of Education, 2001.

Slavkin, Mark, and Lila Crespin. "Rebuilding Arts Education in Urban Schools: Issues and Challenges," *Arts Education Policy Review*, 101(4), March/April 2000.

Smith, Marshall, and Jennifer O'Day. "Systemic School Reform," in Susan Fuhrman and Betty Malen, eds., *Politics of Curriculum and Testing, 1990 Politics of Education Association Yearbook.* New York: Falmer Press, 1990, pp. 233–267.

Smith, Ralph. "The Naked Piano Player: Or What the Rockefeller Report 'Coming to Our Senses' Really Is," *Art Education*, 31(1), January 1978.

Sousa, Suzanne. "Creative Communities: Putting Art at the Heart of Community Building," *Journal of Housing and Community Development*, 61(3), May/June 2004.

Southern Regional Education Board. "Conclusions—Identified Teacher Education Shortage Areas," *2002 Teacher Supply and Demand Study.* Oklahoma City: Oklahoma State Regents for Higher Education, April 2002. As of January 1, 2008: http://www.okhighered.org/studies-reports/teach-supply/conclusions-recommendations.pdf

Stevenson, Lauren M., and Richard J. Deasy. *Third Space: When Learning Matters.* Washington, D.C.: Arts Education Partnership, 2005.

Stone, Clarence, ed. *Changing Urban Education.* Lawrence, Kan.: University of Kansas Press, 1998.

Teitelbaum, Terry, and Stephanie Fuerstner Gillis. *Arts Education: A Review of the Literature.* San Francisco, Calif.: Blueprint Research & Design, Inc., November 2003 (updated February 2004). As of January 1, 2008: http://www.hewlett.org/NR/rdonlyres/0CCCD673-A18D-44FC-B3B6-DA56A4CBD808/0/LiteratureReviewFINAL.pdf

Tushnet, Naida C. *A Guide to Developing Educational Partnerships.* Los Alamitos, Calif.: Southwest Regional Laboratory, October 1993.

von Zastrow, Claus, and Helen Janc. *Academic Atrophy: The Condition of the Liberal Arts in America's Public Schools.* Washington, D.C.: Council for Basic Education, March 2004.

Wakeford, Michael. "A Short Look at a Long Past," in Nick Rabkin and Robin Redmond, eds., *Putting the Arts in the Picture: Reframing Education in the 21st Century.* Chicago, Ill.: Columbia College Chicago, 2004.

Walsh, Kate. "Time in School: Opportunity to Learn," in Chester E. Finn, Jr., and Diane Ravitch, eds., *Beyond the Basics: Achieving a Liberal Education for All Children.* Washington, D.C.: Thomas B. Fordham Institute, July 2007.

West, Martin. "Testing, Learning, and Teaching: The Effects of Test-Based Accountability on Student Achievement and Instructional Time in Core Academic Subjects," in Chester E. Finn, Jr., and Diane Ravitch, eds., *Beyond the Basics: Achieving a Liberal Education for All Children.* Washington, D.C.: Thomas B. Fordham Institute, July 2007.

Winner, Ellen, and Monica Cooper. "Mute Those Claims: No Evidence (Yet) for a Causal Link Between Arts Study and Academic Achievement," *Journal of Aesthetic Education*, 34(3–4), Fall/Winter 2000.

Winner, Ellen, and Lois Hetland. "The Arts in Education: Evaluating the Evidence for a Causal Link," *Journal of Aesthetic Education*, 34(3–4), Fall/Winter 2000.

Woodworth, K. R., H. A. Gallagher, and R. Guha. *An Unfinished Canvas. Arts Education in California: Taking Stock of Policies and Practices. Summary Report.* Menlo Park, Calif.: SRI International, 2007.